N...

Spread your ...s!

love Mum
(x)

11/8/12

Vietnam

NICOLAS CORNET

VIETNAM

A SENSE OF PLACE

Thames & Hudson

CONTENTS

LANDSCAPES AND PADDY FIELDS

Think of Vietnam and your mind is filled with the colour green: sharp, intense, brilliant and thrilling. This greenness will captivate you as you journey from north to south. The rice fields follow you all the way, an endless panorama, a long garland of greenery animated by thousands of figures. Here there are women standing in close lines; over there, men balance on a harrow, shouting commands to their water buffalo. Groups of noisy, laughing villagers are rebuilding a small dyke, and two little girls in a rowing boat are picking water spinach. Timeless visions of a Vietnam that is evolving but which remains predominantly a rural society. The Vietnamese are attached to the land, to the soil; they are aware of its value. They have a saying here: 'A span of land is a span of gold.'

The countryside is not merely a succession of fields, it is a whole world, inhabited not just by people but also by spirits who are respected, revered and feared. Ong Lua is one of the most important, as is Ba Lua, spirit of the paddy field, Son Tinh, spirit of the mountain and Thuy Tinh, spirit of the waters. At the altar, prayers ask the earth for an abundant harvest, aided only by the water buffalo or the oxen.

The countryside also has a profound meaning for the Vietnamese, symbolizing their origins. In Vietnam, people define themselves first and foremost by where they come from: 'Quê o dâu?', 'Where is your land?'. The homeland smells of soil, of rice and water spinach, and when these are shared, this creates a memory and an identity.

The country's own special culture also has a rustic feel. Work songs and shanties, now reproduced in the musical theatre, were once sung in a call and response style by peasants bent double over the rice plants as they transplanted the shoots. Love songs would bring boys and girls together as they worked, their feelings for each other deepening through the time they spent together, their shared tasks and mutual curiosity.

Life in the countryside is controlled by the rhythm of work in the paddy field. Rice is more difficult to cultivate and requires greater care and attention than the cultivation of wheat or corn. The soil and the heavens have to be mastered. When it is the time for ploughing to aerate the ground, the countryside is filled with the sight and sounds of water buffalo and oxen harnessed to farm equipment. The lunar new year is celebrated during the dry season. This is a pleasant period of rest, the start of the marriage season. After the first irrigation, the peasants can be seen wading in the muddy squares, wending their way through the flooded paddy fields. As soon as spring comes, the seed-rice is planted under the watchful eye of the community. Then it is time for transplanting. The women rush into the countryside, and balance like tightrope walkers, up to the knees in mud. Lined up like swallows on a telegraph wire, they advance in serried ranks, carefully planting the precious shoots in the soil. Bent over their work for whole days at a time, shaded by their huge, conical straw hats, they chatter, comment, sing and laugh to their hearts' content.

Irrigation must be carefully regulated. The young shoots need water, but it must be only a few inches deep; too much water will prevent the seedlings from growing, and this will mean transplanting all over again. When the warm sunshine comes in the fifth month, the rice will blossom quickly, helped by the wetness of the flooded fields. Several months of intensive care – weeding and fertilizing – are needed before the ears containing the precious grain make the bright

green plants bend under their weight. When the plants begin to turn yellow, threshing machines are set up in the villages. Men, women and children share the excitement of the harvest. Once the rice has been separated from the stalks, the precious grains are spread out to dry on streets and alleys, roads and squares, and any other dry surface. The heat now becomes a friend, making the grains grow firm and drying the straw so it can be baled into stacks. The scent of rice straw permeates the villages, and the harvest home gladdens hearts.

When the Vietnamese paddy fields are flooded, the people seem to be reflected in the water; when they speak of the fields, they speak of themselves. The shape of their thoughts (echoed in Confucian doctrine), the very essence of their society is structured by the hard work of rice-growing, the back-breaking toil in the tropical humidity, in a heat that coats the body in sweat or in freezing cold that chills to the bone. Their feet wade through the fertile mud, a people whose roots are sunk deep into the earth.

Vietnam is a thoroughly rural society, set in a climate that is typically humid, its landscapes generously watered by rain. Two-thirds of the population work the land and live from farming, rearing animals and harvesting. The everyday struggle to survive has gradually been transformed into a source of income. Throughout the country, food stalls and small restaurants sell dishes freshly prepared on the spot using local ingredients. Offerings include stuffed snails, glazed duck, flowers and vegetables deep-fried in batter, and wild bamboo shoots.

PRECEDING PAGES
North Vietnam: the rice terraces between Moc Chau and Son La.
LEFT
Duck-herding in the Mekong Delta.
RIGHT
Thai girls search for shellfish near Diên Biên Phu.

There is a Vietnamese saying: 'The water buffalo is the beginning of good fortune.' But for families living in the countryside, this animal really is the key to success, because the rice harvest depends on it. The water buffalo is a sturdy beast with short, powerful legs, making it well-suited to work in the thick mud of the flooded fields. The children are responsible for looking after the docile buffalo, and after school they lead them down the country roads. A daily bath helps the animals withstand the oppressive heat.

LEFT
Mekong Delta: a farmer stands on the doorstep of his house on stilts · South Vietnam, Song Bê province: the boys enjoy a bath in pump water which will then be used to water the fields.
RIGHT
North Vietnam: a young buffalo-herder on the road between Lao Cai and Viêt Tri.

In Vietnam, even the urban world has an informal air about it. The smallest courtyard garden makes it possible to reintroduce a touch of nature. Betel shoots climbing a bamboo pole, a mandarin seed taking root, miniature trees: all these plants make themselves at home, and the care with which they are tended is a Buddhist virtue. A life of harmony is achieved through the relationship with the natural world of plants. Second only to raising children, the cultivation of orchids brings a sense of pride at having accomplished something despite the trials and tribulations of life.

LEFT
An inscribed stone stele in a courtyard garden in Hoi An.
RIGHT
Orchids of the genus *Dendrobium*, also known as bamboo orchids.

A common Vietnamese greeting, if you see someone at a mealtime, is '*An com chua?*', which means 'Have you eaten rice yet?' Rice is the basis of the Vietnamese diet. Just the subtle scent of this staple cereal is enough to whet the appetite. If a restaurant were to serve all the types of rice available in each province, the menu would be endless: plain or flavoured white rice, wild red rice, sticky rice with bitter gourd, green rice pressed with bean paste, rice seasoned with palm flowers, sticky yellow-blossom rice, children's rice, happiness rice, steamed rice with coconut milk, rice cooked in the hollow stems of mountain bamboo, fried rice-balls from the Mekong Delta, cubes of rice from Huê, fried rice from Hoi An, rice broth to calm an upset stomach, fermented rice pudding laced with alcohol, and more.

LEFT
Quang Binh province: rice must be washed three times to remove excess starch before cooking.
RIGHT
A family meal consisting of rice, meat or fish is often accompanied by a clear soup (*canh*) and a few boiled vegetables.
• A little girl in the fishermen's district of Nha Trang.

In this lush tropical climate, nature creates a symphony of harmonious colours. The fields and hills are filled with greens of varying shades and intensities, counterpointed by the muted brownish reds of the earth. These reds, darker in dry weather, brighter when wet, seem to give texture to the land, like distant cousins of the earthy browns of Sienna. The clashing colours are strongest where the paths and tracks criss-cross. In shades of ochre, brown and chocolate, the dust coats the faces and hair of travellers. The mud covers the hide of the water buffalo in a rich brown sheen and, in the rainy season, it gives the paddy fields a deep purplish hue.

LEFT
North Vietnam: walking through the six-month-old rice fields in Sa Pa. • South Vietnam: harvesting jasmine flowers for flavouring tea. • North Vietnam: the Sa Pa buffalo-herders riding out to look for grazing land.
RIGHT
Nipa palms. • Woodcut of a water buffalo. • South Vietnam: market gardens near Bao Loc.
INSET
A tiger killed in the Cao Phong region, c. 1907. • A rice-seller in Hanoi, near the Great Lake, c. 1907. • Water buffalo on a banknote. • Ploughing the paddy fields near Hanoi, early twentieth century.

Lotus flowers, the Buddhist symbol of purity, add colour to ponds in the north and south of the country. The many properties of the lotus are used in traditional medicine and as home remedies. The seeds are thought to have a fortifying and calming effect and are used to combat depression. The stalks and leaves are used to staunch bleeding and the stamen filaments are used as a hair dye. Pink or white flowers are left as offerings on altars, and the whole stamens are used to flavour tea in the South. The seeds can be eaten as a snack, or sugar-coated to make sweets.

LEFT
Pink lotus flower in a pond in Huê.
RIGHT
South Vietnam: harvesting lotus roots. These are thinly sliced and often eaten with chopped peanuts, coriander and prawns.

It takes one day in the water, followed by three days in the air, for the rice seed, exposed to the elements, to germinate and become a seedling. The shoots are sown very close together in the sodden earth and soon form a magical green carpet full of promise, nurtured by the family which lavishes special care and attention on it. The young seedlings are planted out by women who stick them into the soft mud in small clumps, an elbow's length apart. The plants will soon merge into long, regular lines that seem to stretch to infinity.

LEFT
North Vietnam: weeding between the seedlings. • Mature rice plants at Sa Pa.
RIGHT
North Vietnam: when working in the open air, the women protect themselves by wearing conical straw hats and scarves to keep out the dust and sun. They consider a pale complexion to be more attractive.

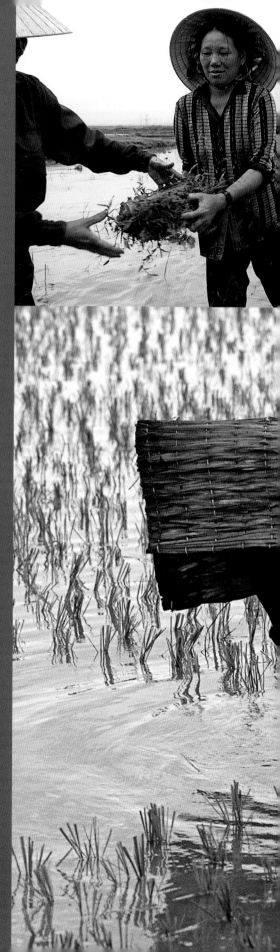

The effects of rain and heat change the appearance of the paddy field. When brown, it is ploughed, harrowed and the seeds are sown; when it turns bright green the seedlings are pricked out and irrigated by the silt-laden water; when golden-yellow, the rice is harvested. The husks left behind after threshing retain their golden colour during winnowing. Finally the ivory grains emerge from their casings, bare and white. Countless and delicate, they trickle through the fingers, giving a sense of abundance.

LEFT
Pricking out the rice seedlings. · Young rice plants on the plain of Thai Binh.
RIGHT
Working in the paddy fields. · Rice-harvesting. · Bent double over the seedlings in the paddy field, a woman pricks out the rice, her back protected by a cape of woven palm leaves. · Grains of rice emerging from the hulling machine.

We would often wander through villages in the countryside, lingering in the fields of ripe rice, sitting at the foot of a tree to admire the immense paddy fields stretching far into the distance; a gust of wind would ruffle the ears of rice and they would move like golden waves while here and there, among the plots of land, clumps of bamboo would rise up like islands decked in greenery, so that we had the impression of sitting beside the sea.

Hoang Ngoc Phach, *A Pure Heart*

RIGHT
Mekong Delta: bathing in
an irrigation channel
beside a paddy field.

The chequerboard of paddy fields is a record of the culture and history of Vietnam. At one time, each field had a specific function. Some provided for the overlords and the local school; others covered administration costs or supported orphanages, widows, or the cult of ancestor worship; sometimes the proceeds were simply donated to the pagoda by the faithful. The fields of the mandarins were given as gifts to those who had rendered services to the king or had honorific titles bestowed upon them.

LEFT
North Vietnam, Ninh Binh province: the paddy fields of Hoa Lu among the sugar-loaf hills.
RIGHT
As protection against sun and rain, the women working in the paddy fields wear capes made of woven palm leaves, giving them a bird-like appearance.

MARKET DAY

The stall-holder shouts 'Banh cuon, Banh chung dai!', as she pushes her bicycle loaded with traditional snacks, such as rice-flour pancakes stuffed with meat or little sticky rice cakes filled with bean sprouts. She passes another woman, carrying a yoke on her shoulders, who is selling shè, a sweet dessert made of tapioca flavoured with sweetcorn or red beans. The market itself is mobile, moving through the streets and alleys, coming at you from all directions. The sellers are chanting and shouting their wares; in the distance, a spoon is being banged on a piece of bamboo to announce that the soup-seller has set up her stall on the corner, selling miên (vermicelli soup); she collects the empty bowls before she moves on.

The market is a lively area whose smoke and smells waft through every door, and fresh vegetables are often delivered by bicycle. Baskets laden with bright green French beans, cabbages and herbs pass by the red brick of an ancient wall, while the deep purple of the aubergines contrasts with the bright yellow walls of a pagoda.

Some markets once stood at the crossroads of important land and river routes, and the wares they sell preserve the memories of the past. Each town and city district has its own market, and all of the major covered markets specialize in particular goods. Fabrics and clothes predominate in one area, cooking utensils and building tools in another; vegetables and flowers are displayed on the pavement, and a separate stall is reserved for the various types of nuoc mam, pungent sauces made from fish and shellfish, often aged and fermented. Nearby are candied fruits and the condiments that the Vietnamese love to use to flavour their noodles, offal and pickles in vinegar.

Hanoi. The covered markets are like caves, and their guardians are tigresses. With their provincial accents and their coarse and colourful vocabulary, they hurl insults at each other amid the fragrances of ginger, garlic and dried fish. Other stall-holders are as silent as shadows, busying themselves with such age-old tasks as delicately encircling rosebuds with a thin thread to prevent them opening too soon, turning back the petals of a lotus-flower bud, or carving miniature toothpicks from bamboo. For a few dongs, agile hands will defy matter and time, applying gaudy make-up to a procession of matronly ladies. In one corner, an elderly woman has set out tiny chairs no higher than a shoe and is selling small cups of bitter tea and single cigarettes. Men patronize her stall, drawing a few puffs on a bamboo pipe of tobacco that is so strong it seems to tear at their lungs. During a lull in trade, the stall-holders devote themselves to their favourite pastime – counting and re-counting their wads of banknotes in delight.

In the open-air markets, canopies are stretched across the narrow streets, like the sails of a ship. Blue or red, opaque or transparent, these strips of cloth provide protection from both the blazing sun and the heavy rain. Moving around requires ducking and dodging. Men and women wander in single file between the rows of stalls, surrounded by meat, fish and vegetables. The market follows the rhythm of the city – you can feel its pulse here. At dawn it is slow; by ten o'clock in the morning it is bustling and busy; by noon it is overheated and suffocating. Then as evening falls and the setting sun extends its long purple tongues of shadow over the stretched canvas of the awnings, it explodes back into life again.

As is the case in every country where good food is appreciated, the markets are popular places for both shopping and eating. In Ho Chi Minh City (formerly Saigon), in the Cho Cu or Old Market, the little stalls that line the edges of the large market hall are redolent with the wonders of Vietnamese cuisine. There are tiny *cha gio* (spring rolls) and little glazed brochettes, known as *miên*, flavoured with coriander leaves. The sellers call out their wares, inviting customers to taste their snacks, surrounded by the fragrance of dumplings and *banh xeo*, omelettes filled with soya beans and prawns.

The market is a voyage in itself, a hymn to taste and flavour. The scents of star anise and liquorice combine with lemongrass, ginger and coriander. Brilliant tropical fruits catch the eye, their brightly coloured skins full of delicate flesh: mangoes, dragon fruit, lychees, longans, jackfruit, custard apples, guavas, papayas and starfruit.

'Sticky rice, who wants some sticky rice ...?'
'Cakes, come and taste my lovely cakes...!'
Each stall-holder had her own chant, with its trills and low rumblings. In our neighbourhood alone, there were seven sticky-rice vendors. You could recognize each one... it was the first music of my childhood. Each morning, my mother scurried about, tidying her display of foodstuffs and snacks. She piled them up helter-skelter, until they overflowed the baskets, everything: dried bamboo shoots, rice crisps, and wheat crackers, Chinese cellophane noodles and Vietnamese vermicelli, soybeans, red beans, black beans, peanuts, raw sesame seeds, husked...

Duong Thu Huong, *The Paradise of the Blind*

38

40

In Hanoi, the 36 Guilds district is the heart of the Old Quarter, but no guidebook will tell you the best addresses. The knowledge is spread by word of mouth, between family members or from friend to friend. People recommend the best places to each other, though they do not always tell all. Succulent glazed pork, an importer of fish sauce from Huê, a particularly skilled craftsman, a repairer you can trust: these trade secrets are dispensed carefully and in small quantities, like all good advice.

LEFT
Hanoi: plastic sandals for sale.
RIGHT
Hanoi: a stall selling glazed duck and pork in a street in the 36 Guilds district.

In the side-streets of Hanoi and Ho Chi Minh City, the markets are open every day. Vietnamese cuisine relies on many vegetables, fruits and herbs that need to be eaten fresh, the same day on which they were picked. Women of the city hurry to the market every morning to do the day's shopping. The carrots, potatoes, salad greens, radishes, cabbages, tomatoes and strawberries that are typical of temperate climates are grown at high altitude and brought in daily. The stalls also trade in more exotic vegetables, such as water spinach, bamboo shoots, beansprouts, sweet potatoes, cassava, taro, and more.

LEFT
Patterned ceramic dishes for sale in Hoi An. • Vegetable market in the Da Kao district of Ho Chi Minh City.
RIGHT
The Tay Nguyên Market in Tonkin, *c.* 1906. • A traditional Vietnamese woodcut design. • North Vietnam: Bac Ha market.
INSET
The fruit market in Saigon, *c.* 1914. • Market in Tonkin, *c.* 1907. • Coins and a banknote.

GIẤY MỘT ĐỒNG VÀNG

HANOI

44

South Medicine Street and North Medicine Street in Hanoi. The traditional pharmacopoeia derives its properties from a wide variety of remedies to maintain the 'flow of life'. The prevailing concept is that there is no such thing as illness, only imbalances that can be reversed with the help of the right medicinal plants. Cinnamon and cloves are considered antibacterial, eucalyptus works to fight intestinal infections, rose-apple leaves are beneficial for the lungs and windpipe, betel leaves are good for eczema, and star anise and ginger relieve stomach pain.

LEFT
Hanoi: traditional medicines sold wholesale.
RIGHT
South Vietnam: ducks for sale in a country market.

In Vietnam, goods can be transported in a huge variety of ways: in backpacks or on the shoulders, on bicycles or motor scooters. Fruits and vegetables can be loaded onto a yoke (above left) and taken onto buses and ferries, and even up stairs. A hammock stretched on bamboo poles between two bicycles becomes a rural ambulance (far right, above), making it possible to ride along the tops of the dykes between paddy fields, where a vehicle with two wheels in the front would be too wide to get through. A double-decker rack covered in chicken-wire becomes a hen house for delivering live birds (left). A bamboo frame can be used for hanging all types of plastic household utensils and cookware to be sold in the narrow streets (right). Ingenuity is used to solve any problem, no matter how simple or complicated.

OVERLEAF
This grocer's shop on a boat made of woven bamboo moves over the water to visit customers who live on the river.

46

Vietnamese hats are often made of palm leaves stretched over a bamboo frame. Those owned by men and soldiers were once reinforced with metal at the pointed crown. Women's hats were once a different shape, with a raised edge, flat underside and a chin-strap. These were often decorated with designs or poems written in the ancient ideogram script, and adorned with paper flowers or brightly coloured lace. Conical straw hats are light but sturdy, making it easy to move and work while staying shaded from the sun and protected from the rain.

LEFT
The flower market in Dông Xuan, Hanoi.
RIGHT
Fruit-seller near the East Gate in Hanoi. • Hanoi, the Great Lake: Tonkinese coolies in 1907.

Nature here creates complicated and clever sorbets...
The mango tastes of sour milk at first, then of apricot,
then of a hint of turpentine. But a really ripe mango does
not taste of sour milk. From the very start, it has the flavour
of a delicate jelly, an apricot with the subtleties of a peach.
And, at the very end, the turpentine flavour is sublimated,
idealized, remaining chemical no longer, but as delicate as
the taste of vanilla. The mangosteen has the charms of a
sherbet from *A Thousand and One Nights*... Its skin is
reminiscent of a bronze or earthenware pot.
When this austere shell is cut with a knife, it reveals a
sphere of white sorbet encased in pale pink Chinese
porcelain. And the flavour is that of a sorbet,
touched with the barest hint of lemon.

Léon Werth, *Cochinchine*

Fruit holds a special place in Vietnamese daily life. It is considered good manners to bring fruits for your hosts when on a family visit. Old people and children love them, and their high vitamin content and nutritious sweetness mean they are healthy for all. According to traditional belief, fruits are divided into two categories: those that are reputed to cool the body by reducing its internal temperature (yin), and those which increase the body temperature (yang). Apples, mandarins and mangosteens are considered to be 'cold' fruit, while mangoes, durians and jackfruit are 'hot'.

LEFT
The Hang Da Market in Hanoi.
RIGHT
Aubergines and starfruit on a market stall in Hanoi.

LIFE ON
THE WATER

According to legend, a mother dragon once came down from the sky to help the Vietnamese people chase away invaders. In the Bay of Along, the humps of its long back can still be seen in the form of grey mounds of rock, polished and smoothed by time, worn away by wind and rain.

These islands have evocative names, some based on their shapes, some poetic or linked to local legends. They include Fortress Island, Incense-Burner Island, Surprise Island, Marvel Island, Puppet Island, Monkey Island, and Fighting Cock Island.

In the Cove of Stars, near the Toad Seaway, halfway between the open sea and the port of Hon Gai, fishermen and their families are gathered into a floating village. As soon as evening falls, junks and sampans converge to form improvised clusters, sheltered behind the huge rocks, safe from storms, ill winds and pirates. Today, the wooden homes of the fishermen are moored throughout the year and attached to floats. The village of Cua Van whiles away peaceful hours on a jade sea. Day and night, gently rolling and pitching, the fishing community follows the rhythm of the seasons and the tides.

It is seven o'clock in the morning. The big fishing boats have already left their harbour, piercing the silence and cool of the night, heading for the open sea. Between the sugar-loaf islands, little girls row their lightweight boat from their home to the school in the heart of the village.

Thanh, aged twelve, vigorously beats the taut skin of his drum, calling the pupils to morning lessons. The beats build to a crescendo, and soon echo throughout the village, the sound reflecting off the rocks that protect Cua Van from the swell of the open sea. In the space of a few minutes, on the dark and sleepy waves, dozens of woven bamboo craft, made watertight with pitch, emerge from nowhere, hastening to the centre of the floating village. Manipulating the heavy oars, schoolbags at their feet, the children converge on the floating school, shouting and laughing.

On deck, Miss Trinh and Miss Phuong, who teach their young charges regardless of wind and

" " Many of the children from this floating village have never set foot on land"

tide, are brushing their hair, dreamily gazing into the distance. They smile at the sight of their high-spirited pupils rowing in their direction. One by one, the rowing boats draw up alongside the school. The children tie them to the gangway and leap on to the platform that serves as a playground and exercise yard in front of the classroom. They lower their eyes and respectfully greet their teacher with 'Chao Cô' – 'Good morning, auntie'.

At the signal, they sit at their plastic tables, just above the water that shimmers through the gaps in the floorboards. Their exercise books open, their young eyes are riveted to the blackboard. Miss Trinh and Miss Phuong enter the classroom and are greeted with a chorus of children's voices as rhythmic as the chants in the pagoda.

At break time, the children jostle each other on the platform; a few of them jump into their boats 'to go for a row' under the amused gaze of Miss Phuong. They are swift and skilful at manoeuvring their bamboo skiffs and handle the oars and rudder with dexterity. 'Many of them have never set foot

on land,' explains the teacher. 'The other day, one of them asked "What does a bicycle look like?"' The tumult grows louder when Miss Khoa's floating grocery pulls alongside. Miss Trinh buys a few vegetables, oil and a bottle of fish sauce. The children are attracted by the biscuits and sweets on display, staring in wide-eyed wonder.

Finally, after class, a flotilla of rowing boats full of chattering children sail homewards before darkness falls.

Miss Phuong corrects the children's schoolbooks while she sips green tea and prepares her lessons for the following day. The flame of the oil lamp flickers and she glances outside as the night darkens. In the distance, the lamps on the fishing boats are lit, one by one, reflecting off the cliffs and casting strange shadows. The pages of the notebooks flutter as the wind rises over the Bay of Along.

Golden sunlight bathes the waters of the Bay of Along in the autumn. Across the bay, the typhoons have died down, the waters have ceased roaring and the wind no longer whips up the waves. Everyone, young and old, has been mobilized for the last good fishing trips of the season; the wooden boats set out for the open sea, to the island of Hainan. Soft light fills the Gulf of Tonkin, giving the villages, cliffs and coves a warm glow that marks the end of the festive season, before the onset of winter.

PRECEDING PAGES
Sheltered by the rocks of the Jade Mountain, the floating village of Van Gia overlooks the Cua Van pass.
LEFT
The port of Hon Gai, in the Bay of Along: the fishermen deliver the night's catch to the fish market.
RIGHT
Early in the morning, still wearing his cotton pyjamas, Mr Khanh leaves to cast his fishing rod just outside the village.

Beneath their floating homes in the Bay of Along, families set up fish farms. Cage-like nets are extended beneath the planks of the jetty. Young fish caught by the fishermen or bought from sellers are placed in this keeping net. Catfish and red mullet, whose flesh is highly prized, are able to grow here, safe from predators; this is how the fishermen overcome a shortage of income in the winter and during poor seasons. The farmed fish sell for a good price, giving the families a regular source of income and saving them from having to resort to loans if money is tight in the family.

LEFT
North Vietnam: a fisherman is drawing in the net he has dragged behind his woven bamboo boat.
RIGHT
Villagers buy small fry from wholesalers, and use them as food for the farmed fish.

The sea is now in darkness. A few sparse lanterns still burn on the junks lying at anchor. In the middle of the cove, the only bright spot is the flickering light from the door of the customs house. On the right, there is a glimmer of light from the thatched huts. And flickering in the sky, the moving milky way of a lighthouse. As I lie in my bunk – how mild these nights seem to me as the breeze blows from the open sea after those stifling nights in the Delta! – I fritter away my thoughts in all of the scattered sounds. I listen to life on the junks. The women traders, in their little sampans like floating cradles under their straw roofs, travel from ship to ship, crying their wares in the form of fruit, toasted rice and other delicacies. The shouts move away, draw nearer, mingle... in the stern of each sampan a kid is rowing.

Roland Dorgelès, *On the Mandarin Road*

Eleven o'clock in the morning. The uniformed schoolchildren leave their floating school and head for home. They row themselves in woven bamboo skiffs that are light, flexible and sturdy. The boats are coated with a type of lacquer, made from tree resin according to an ancient recipe, which makes them watertight and prevents barnacles from growing on the hull. As soon as children learn to walk, they learn to row, proudly copying the movements of the other children and their parents.

LEFT
A Vietnamese girl in school uniform. Girls wear a white blouse and blue pinafore dress, while boys wear a white shirt and blue trousers.
RIGHT
The floating village of Cua Van in the Bay of Along.

The village of Cua Van is busy. Miss Khoa's floating grocery store zigzags between the homes, offering villagers the latest wares. The fishermen repair their nets, the children finish eating their sticky rice balls and begin to get ready for school. The women who farm pearl oysters straighten their uniforms and say a last few words to their children. The provisions boat bringing fresh water enters the village, blowing a powerful blast on its foghorn.

LEFT
Fishermen at rest in the cove of the village of Cua Van. • A Chinese junk in the Bay of Along, c. 1906. • Detail of a village temple, from an old woodcut. • Plastic shoes belonging to the children. • At about 6.30 am, Mrs Vê goes to the centre of the cove that houses the village. This is where the shuttle boat picks up the women who work on the oyster farms.

INSET
Sampan at the foot of a sugar-loaf hill, c. 1914. • A junk at anchor, c. 1907. • Life on a sampan in the port of Hon Gai. • A traditional image of a carp.

RIGHT
Once a week, the villagers of Cua Van do their shopping in the port of Hon Gai.

Sunday is the longest day in Cua Van. As soon as the sun rises, the children get together to play in their rowing boats or do some fishing. At about nine in the morning, courting couples in their best clothes discreetly head for the nearest rocks, hoping for some privacy. People go on visits and a few make for the port. Karaoke songs fill the air, mingling with the laughter of children. When night falls, children and parents gather on the threshold of Mrs Vê's house in front of the TV set. She has rented a video cassette in Hon Gai, so it's film night in Cua Van.

LEFT
On the gangway in front of the school, young Hau proudly shows off her pink sweater, her Sunday best.
RIGHT
Family dinner on a small boat.
OVERLEAF
Miss Huong, one of the local teachers, buys vegetables and fruit from the floating shop.

For him, as for Sinh and some of the fishermen, this bay is a city. The cliffs are his palaces, temples and houses; the exposed reefs are like monuments. Just as streets are lined with homes, so the rock walls rise up on each side of the waterways. Everywhere, there are avenues, boulevards, esplanades or curving alleys. If the sea has replaced the paved roadway, could it be because the land suddenly sank, as the fishermen claim? The water level rose, half-submerging the town. Before it was invaded by the waves, spirits had made their home there. Ky has heard that sampan owners sometimes find mysterious marvels, submerged treasures, deep in the coves. Perhaps this is why they are drawn to the endless meanders of this unique city.

Yvonne Schultz, *Le Sampanier de la baie d'Along*
(The Sampan-Owner of the Bay of Along)

LEFT
A family of fishermen living on
their moored houseboat.

Mrs Ngoc is the only seamstress in Cua Van. Since the village has no electricity supply, she uses pedal power to sew, hem and mend. Her Chinese sewing machine is just a copy of the old Singer treadle machines, but it does the job. Waistcoats, *ao dai* (traditional Vietnamese tunic dresses) and uniforms are all pieced together and fitted. When a boat passes, her home rocks. Mrs Ngoc stops pedalling for a moment and stares into the distance. The rolling waters rock her little girl and her husband, who are resting. Tonight her husband will go out fishing in the open sea. In Cua Van, lives follow the rhythm of the tides.

LEFT
Inside Mrs Ngoc's floating home in Cua Van.
RIGHT
Hoi and Ba begin their homework as soon as they get home from school.

The school is moored to the rocks, as are the other floating homes. At the approach of a typhoon, the fishermen tow the school deep inside the cove to protect it from the sea swell and storm winds. Five groups of children fill the two classrooms in shifts every day. Miss Phuong, the teacher, begins by reading aloud to her pupils, barely disturbed by the cries of the passing seagulls. Then she gets the children to sing; after this, lessons start, paced by a few taps of the ruler. Through a window with no glass, she looks out at the houses, ships and cliffs.

LEFT
A siesta in a hammock. • Miss Phuong, the teacher. • Dong is doing his homework in the staff room. • Heading for home. • Scribbling a note at the end of the school day.
RIGHT
The living room of Mrs Ha's floating home. • Son, aged thirteen, is a fisherman already. He lives on the boat with his mother and young brother.

A wedding on the water. Overnight, the guests gath- at the bride's house. Two li sailing boats leave the still- sleeping village of Cua Van slipping between the sugar loaf rocks. On the boat, the bridesmaids put on their make-up in the pale light o dawn, just before mooring Hung Than, where Thanh, bride, lives. Welcomed by h future in-laws, Thang, the bridegroom, presents his intended with a bouquet of roses. After a short ceremo and some photographs, the Cua Van villagers sail home bringing the bride with the In the bridegroom's modes house, decorated with pale blue satin, with red lantern that represent happiness, a traditional seven-course meal is served to the diners including tasty red mullet as the centrepiece. In the evening, the families take t. leave. At the age of twenty- two, Thanh prepares to spe her first night on a floating home in Cua Van.

LEFT
A wedding photo hangs above the ti
on Mr Loc's boat.
RIGHT
The bride in white and her bridesma
in red arrive in sight of the village of
Van Gia.

TEMPLES
AND PAGODAS

The kneeling woman makes a deep obeisance, her forehead touching the ground, before the altar of the pagoda. She has bought fruit, joss sticks, a few flowers and a flask of rice wine to present on a large round tray with a few banknotes as an offering to the monks; then she lights the joss stick and whispers a litany of prayers that she learned from her grandmother. Clutching the joss sticks, her hands clasped over her forehead, she prays to the Buddha, the spirits and her family ancestors. She performs this ritual on the anniversaries of her ancestors' deaths, on the first and fifteenth days of the Buddhist calendar, and on the occasion of the lunar New Year and other festivals. Sometimes she does it simply because she feels the need.

In Vietnamese homes, the altar dedicated to the spirit of the house faces the entrance. The altar to the ancestors has its own special place in the house. It often covers a whole wall, even if the family has modest means and there is only one mat on which to eat and sleep. In wealthier families, a whole room is set aside for the veneration of ancestors; sometimes a pagoda is built outside the family home in their honour.

Souls are cared for, spirits cherished, and memories preserved in this land that has been so often ravaged by invasions and wars, famines, floods and plagues. One by one, the great religions, doctrines and spiritual philosophies have made their mark on this land, which is infused with magic and spirituality. Monks and pedlars, missionaries, merchants, colonists and adventurers all brought with them their own spiritual practices and concepts. The representatives of global faiths have embraced local traditions and respected the local deities, trying to add their own message rather than claiming to replace them.

Priests, seekers of the souls of the dead, fortune-tellers, shamans from the mountains, monks and hermits: all of these spiritual figures share the ills and joys of daily life. Consulted by the villagers, country folk and city-dwellers in both north and

Wandering souls,
will you ever find deliverance?"

south, they are considered a valuable source of advice. In this corner of the earth torn asunder by history, they create a unity within the country, a harmony of souls.

In the south of Vietnam, freedom of worship made it possible for minority faiths and syncretic sects to be born. Cao Dai, Hoa Hao, and various Buddhist sects saw the first light of day in the plains between the wide branches of the Mekong river. Rituals were copied or created, holy places were decreed, symbolism formulated and practices initiated that set the pace of daily life as season followed season.

In the north, in the *dinh*, the communal village houses, altars are built to ancestors and other spirits whose greatness and mercy governs the lives and actions of all the inhabitants. Fishing and farming, war and travel, health and prosperity are all subject to forces that are venerated, respected and feared. In the streets of old Hanoi, spirit money and 'hell notes' are bought and burned as offerings to the spirits, and, on the banyan trees dedicated to wandering souls, incense can always be seen burning and votive offerings dance in the wind.

As for the faithful of central Vietnam, all that keeps them on the ground is the thick mud of the paddy fields. History has seen the emperors of Huê boast that they have a divine mandate and raise their court geomancers to the rank of ministers. Those who claim descent from the sovereigns visit the temples and tombs in secret, offering incantations and prayers for the protection and good fortune of their family line.

In the countryside and in the towns, the temples are visited daily. Religious buildings play an important role in the life of the Vietnamese. They provide a link to the divine, to the ancestors and the dead. Altars are set up at the entrances to pagodas and communal houses and at the foot of the ancient banyans (*Ficus benghalensis*), since these mighty trees are believed to be inhabited by spirits.

PRECEDING PAGES
Hanoi: Temple of the White Horse (Bach Ma), the oldest in the capital. The wall of the first courtyard contains plaster mouldings representing the legend of a fish that changed into a dragon.

LEFT
The One-Pillar Pagoda (Chua Mot Cot) in Hanoi is often considered to be a symbol of the city. It was built after the king, Ly Thai Tô, saw in a dream an image of a goddess on a lotus flower. A stele records that 'a stone column was erected in the middle of Lake Linh Chieu which supported a thousand-petal lotus resting on a red pagoda.'

RIGHT
Hoi An: the Temple of Ong, dedicated to Quan Cong, built in the Chinese quarter.

92

At the start of every ceremony, incense is burned so that the fragrant smoke will accompany the prayer that rises to the other world. The lower part of the joss sticks is dyed in a bright colour, green, red or yellow. The joss sticks are stuck in a vase filled with sand or ashes. The upper part is coated with a fragrant paste, containing benzoin resin or similar substances. In the light that filters into the pagoda, the perfumes mingle – citronella, sandalwood, cardamom, rose and lotus.

LEFT
Spiral joss sticks and candles lit as offerings in the Pagoda of the Jade Emperor (Ngoc Hoang) in the Da Kao district of Ho Chi Minh City.
RIGHT
Joss sticks, ready to be used as offerings.
· A worshipper in a pagoda in Cholon, the Chinese district of Ho Chi Minh City.
OVERLEAF
Before setting out on a fishing trip, the Tran family opens the curtain covering the altar of their ancestors. The incense sticks and *lai* (prostrations) are believed to bring protection and prosperity, a safe trip and an abundant catch, everything the family wishes for.

In Vietnam, the majority religion, Buddhism, co-exists with traditional ancestor worship. The faith came from India by land to the north and by sea to the south, and embraced influences from animism, Taoism and Confucianism as it took root in Vietnamese soil. The Catholic community has a strong presence, both in the big cities and in some of the southern regions. Islam is also represented. An unusual feature of Vietnam is that it has developed its own minority faiths based on Buddhism (Hoa Hao), syncretic cults such as Cao Dai, and small sects such as the Coconut Cult and the Whale Cult. These co-exist with local worship of tutelary or family spirits, goddesses and fairies. Ancestors and wandering souls are also revered; no one is forgotten.

LEFT
Hoi An: roof of a pagoda. • Traditional woodcut of a temple. • The Tay Ninh Holy See, centre of the Cao Dai faith.
INSET
The One-Pillar Pagoda, Hanoi, c. 1907. • Interior of a pagoda in Cholon in the early twentieth century. • Entrance to the Pagoda of Gratitude, Tonkin. • A packet of joss sticks.
RIGHT
North Vietnam, Ninh Binh province: ceremony in the courtyard of Phat Diem Cathedral. • The Central Mosque built in Saigon in 1935 by Muslims from South India.

Life in the pagodas is organized around prayer times. Seated on a mat facing a statue of the Buddha, a priest recites the sutras. He regularly punctuates the prayers by hitting a hollow, reverberating piece of wood with a hammer, then taps a bronze bell. The litanies rise among the columns of red-lacquered ironwood in the main sanctuary. The worshippers repeat part of the incantations in chorus. As they recite the sutras, they invoke the female deity Quan Am, to ward off danger or attract the blessings of fertility.

LEFT
Ba Da Pagoda, Hanoi: beating a wooden plank with her mallet, a priestess calls the priests to mealtime.
RIGHT
A young trainee priest in the courtyard of the Thiên Mu Pagoda in Huê.

Our visit to the pagoda was in deference to a
principle no different from that followed in the Moi
villages. We were being presented to the tutelary spirit.
The pagoda of a tutelary spirit is to be found in every
Vietnamese village, and sometimes there are two or more.
In the past the ancient cult has been modified by the system
of Confucius and by Buddhism but now the driving force
in the two great philosophies has faltered and waned,
and the cult still survives. The tutelary spirit was once
some outstanding personality, or even its founder,
for whom, in return for services rendered, has been
created a sort of spiritual baronetcy.

Norman Lewis, *A Dragon Apparent*

RIGHT
The Temple of Literature (Van Mieu),
in Hanoi. Young art students draw details
of a stele which stands on the back of a
carved turtle. On the stele are engraved
the names of honoured scholars.

Votive and ritual objects, often made of paper, are reminders of possessions that were favourites of the deceased: a motorcycle, cigarettes, clothing, crockery, furniture. Fake banknotes or 'spirit notes' will help him or her negotiate with the guardians of the other world. In addition to these offerings, there are cardboard representations of living people, pets and servants to faithfully accompany the deceased. To commemorate the anniversaries of deaths, and on some other festivals, these representations are consigned to the flames in front of the deceased's former home in the living world.

LEFT
Spirit money for sale in the Cholon market, in the Chinese district of Ho Chi Minh City. • Ho Chi Minh City, Da Kao district: representation of a spirit in the Pagoda of the Jade Emperor.
RIGHT
Joss sticks. • The Quan Thanh Pagoda in Hanoi. • Joss sticks spread out to dry. • Offerings at the altar of a pagoda in Hon Gai. • Altar on a rice-barge in the Mekong Delta.

During the Tết Festival – the lunar New Year celebration – and the Buddhist festivals of the first and fifteenth day of the lunar month, a crowd converges on the pagodas. Prosperity, happiness, longevity, fertility: prayers are offered for all these things, on behalf of family members, friends and colleagues. Carrying their joss sticks high on their foreheads, the faithful move from room to room, and at each stopping point they place a few smoking joss sticks from their bundle into a vase. Every time a gift of money is donated to the pagoda, a gong or drum is sounded. Consecrated oils are burned to help the granting of wishes and once consecrated, the offerings are taken home to bring luck to the household.

LEFT
The Tết Festival at the Thiên Hau Pagoda in Cholon, the Chinese quarter of Ho Chi Minh City.
RIGHT
Little altar in front of a house in Cholon.

Incense is used in ceremonies to honour the Buddha, tutelary spirits, ancestors and the dead. Worshippers give offerings of fruits and flowers, light three joss sticks, and prostrate themselves five times. These numbers are symbolic – three represents the Three Jewels of Buddhism: the Buddha, the Dharma and the Sangha; five represents the Five Poisons: ignorance, greed, hatred, pride and jealousy. Votive papers are suspended from the coils of incense, inscribed with wishes written in Chinese characters by the pagoda's scribe. The coils will burn for three weeks, giving time for the wishes to be granted.

LEFT
A devotee lights a coil of incense in a pagoda.
RIGHT
Coils of incense hanging in the Thiên Hau Pagoda.

As a free person I can always come and go,
Not caught in ideas of being and non-being.
Let your steps be leisurely.
Waxing or waning, the moon is always the moon.
The wind is still flying. Can you feel it, my dear?
Bringing the rain from afar to nourish the nearby cloud.
Drops of sunshine fall from on high to earth below
and the lap of earth touches the clear vault of sky.

Thich Nhat Hanh, *No Death, No Fear*

LEFT
South Vietnam: Buddhist priests
returning from a village.

Buddhism reached Vietnam by two routes. Theravada Buddhism arrived from the south with the merchants who came to the country by land and sea from Thailand, Burma and Ceylon. Mahayana Buddhism came from the north, originating from India and Nepal via China.

PEOPLE OF THE MOUNTAINS

115

Hmong women walk in single file on top of the embankments, looking like brightly coloured dots amid the rice terraces. With an indigo blue apron thrown over their red-bordered dresses, they dress in colours that contrast strikingly with the emerald green of the rice plants in the paddy fields.

In the high valleys of North Vietnam, the hill tribes of the Hmong, Yao and Tai cling to the mountainsides like the clouds and mists. Once horsemen who rode the forgotten steppes, they have exchanged their whips for walking sticks to help them climb the steep slopes and ploughs to make furrows in the paddy fields. They were once nomads, but were driven out of their lands by war or famine, and it is here that they have settled down. Fleeing the humid plains and swamps inhabited by the Kinh (the Vietnamese ethnic majority), they ceased their wanderings. They gradually conquered and cultivated acre after acre, in the valleys of Miên Bac (North Vietnam), close to the Chinese frontier.

They carved the mountains into protective walls and fashioned their new kingdom into huge terraces of green fields, building up dykes, diverting streams, dredging the silt and bringing in fresh water to cultivate rice and maize. On the leeward sides of the mountains, by the river springs, they built their villages.

The names of these peoples sound almost onomatopaeic: Hmong, Tai, Yao (or Dao), Nung. Their traditional garments are like miniature landscapes that record stories, arouse curiosity and provoke questions. The long circular skirts of the Flowered Hmong women, edged with crimson borders, are decorated with batik prints. Do these complicated patterns reproduce the secret plans of their ancestral strongholds? Are those genuine coins used as fastenings on the women's blouses? Were they once part of a treasure trove? What is the origin of their embroidery patterns, the brightly coloured waves that climb their necks and shoulders and encircle their wrists?

For these peoples without a nation, their clothing is their flag of distinction, a standard by which their identity is created and affirmed. Their colours are a proud part of their names: the Black Hmong and Flowered Hmong, the Black Tai and

**❝ ❝ Fish swim in the water,
birds fly in the air,
the Hmong live in the mountains"**

White Tai, and the Red Yao. The women, princesses of their mist-shrouded kingdom, deck themselves in these bright hues.

Linen, cotton and wool are carded, spun and wound at communal evening gatherings. The thread is woven by women working at home. When they go to the hemp fields, the young girls break the stalks and roll the fibres into balls; once these have been softened (or retted), the strands will be woven and made into jackets and leggings to protect the calves against the leeches that live in the water. Dyes are extracted from fruit and roots. In front of each house, there are vats of indigo in which the hemp cloth is soaked.

In many communities, embroidered cloth is part of the trousseau; a young girl's skill is judged by how finely she embroiders. Girls of marriageable age therefore display their dexterity and creativity in their work, and future mothers-in-law will try to read the future of their sons in the embroidery, just as soothsayers look for omens.

In the Bac Ha market, stalls are stacked with coloured braids and bright sewing threads. The Hmong girls cannot resist their allure, and the place becomes a huge and creative pageant of embroidery and batik, prints and plain cloth. Although the people of the plains, subjected to so many outside influences, have now abandoned their traditional costumes, these garments have found a refuge among the hill tribes.

Richly decorated umbrellas also serve as sunshades for the women as they walk across slopes and peaks to go gathering, hunting, shopping or visiting their families on festive occasions. With collars that rise high at the nape of the neck, even the fanciest costumes serve as protection from the leeches that might drop from the top of the curving bamboo stalks and the branches that arch over the forest paths.

As the shifting colours of their dresses disappear into the surrounding greenery, the women can still be heard as they move away, their metallic jewelry clinking with every step.

120

More than twenty hill tribes inhabit the mountainous north of Vietnam. The Hmong, Yao (or Dao), Tai and Nung peoples live on the left bank of the Red River, while the Thai and Muong people are mostly to be found on the right bank, as far as the Ma and Ca rivers. Each community has its own lifestyle and preferred dwelling place. Some villages are located high up on the steep slopes of the mountains, while others are to be found in the valleys. It is difficult to date the origin of these ethnic peoples. At Sa Pa, huge blocks of carefully engraved stone have been found, covered in decorative patterns that have been attributed to the early Stone Age period.

PRECEDING PAGES
The lands of the Black Hmong lie near Sa Pa, in the Mong La river valley.
LEFT
A Red Yao woman returning home to her village.
RIGHT
Girls of the Flowered Hmong in Bac Ha.

Sa Pa still holds its famous Love Market, where young Hmong people come in search of a kindred spirit. This is an age-old tradition whereby girls and boys can meet and spend part of the night talking, singing and laughing. Some of them play a musical accompaniment to their courtship on a bamboo mouth-harp, a traditional Hmong instrument. At one time, the marriage rituals of the Hmong community were much cruder. During the night, the chosen woman would be simply abducted by having a blanket thrown over her and she would be taken to the house of the suitor. During the weeks following this abduction, the families would cement the union through dowries and gifts negotiated according to custom.

LEFT AND RIGHT
Young people of the Red Yao walking from Lao Cai to Pho Rang.

That day, I found myself in the Muong-La market. It is an open-air market, quite bustling, where a wide range of items are sold – a whole world of junk – and where a variety of hill tribes mingle. Young Tai and Xa girls come to sell their peaches, plums and quinces picked in the forest. The Hmong come in a group, men and women, with their hair tightly pulled into a bun and their baskets filled with anonas, morinda roots and a type of sticky rice known as mountain rice, found only on the high plateaux of North Vietnam, whose grains are such bright red that they look as if they have been dipped in a bath of dye, rice that is particularly sticky and fragrant. And everywhere there are row upon row of items imported from China: cloth printed with floral patterns, Thermos flasks, saucepans, plates, and heaven knows what else.

Nguyên Huy Thiep, *Conte d'amour un soir de pluie* (Love Story on a Rainy Evening)

In front of a Black Hmong house, pieces of hemp and linen are being soaked in a bath of indigo dye. The dye is obtained from the roots of a plant which the men gather in the forest. The women excel in making it into garments which they weave on simple wooden-framed looms. In between toiling in the fields, they move the shuttles to and fro over the pedal-driven loom. From the lengths of cloth they cut leggings, skirts, shawls, blouses and caps, which give the men, with their long-barrelled rifles slung on their backs, a piratical air as they work in the paddy fields.

LEFT
Tai woman near Diên Biên Phu. • Hmong child near Sa Pa.
RIGHT
Weaving the hemp into cloth in a Hmong house near Sa Pa. • Dyeing with indigo in a Hmong village near Sa Pa. • Drying indigo-dyed cloth. • Hmong women near Lao Cai.
INSET
Children on a village bridge at Lang Can, Tonkin, c. 1907. • Nung women in the village of Nan Nhung, Tonkin, c. 1907. • Vietnamese stamps featuring various hill tribes.

The Hmong people are divided into several subgroups that are found in around ten provinces in North Vietnam, Laos, China and Myanmar, scattered throughout the Himalayan foothills. Green Hmong (Xanh), Red Hmong (Do), Flowered Hmong (Hoa), Black Hmong (Den) and White Hmong (Der) settled more than two centuries ago in northern Tonkin. Their homes are very simple, consisting of a main room built around the hearth and one or two bedrooms with beaten earth floors. The upper level is used to store grain to keep it dry and as a place for farm tools and household equipment. When a family event is taking place, a bunch of leaves is placed on the wooden fence outside. This warns visitors or strangers to be on their way, for fear that they may bring bad luck to the family.

LEFT
Market day in Bac Ha.
RIGHT
Near Son La: a Black Tai child in ceremonial dress.
OVERLEAF
Flowered Hmong women, selling cloth in Bac Ha Market.

132

The Yao people love red. The women cover their foreheads, shaven temples and chignons with a large turban, tied at the front. Antique coins and little bells are sewn around the edge; the jingling is reputed to frighten away the spirits that haunt the forest paths. Little red woollen pompoms are fixed around their necks and long red tassels fall down their backs, over the multicoloured embroidery on the jackets. The patterns enclosed in the embroidered squares are mainly derived from the animal or vegetable kingdom, although motifs such as farm tools, human figures and letters are sometimes added.

LEFT
The Yao could once be recognized by their distinctive headdress, made from hair coated in wax, sometimes mixed with dried squash fibres sewn together (early twentieth-century photograph).
RIGHT
Detail of Hmong embroidery. • A Red Yao woman at Sa Pa market.

Collars are all completely covered in patterns, embroidered in all kinds of shapes and colours, so that it is hard to make out the original colour of the cloth; the sleeves are also covered in multicoloured strips of cloth, sewn in braid-like rows from wrist to elbow. In some tribes, boys can be just as decorated as the girls. Among the White Miao, the skirts are decorated only with pleats, but in most of the other tribes they disappear under coloured embroidery, batik patterns and many multicoloured pieces of appliqué fabric. Leggings, which are from 10 to 15 metres long, are always white, and aprons are dyed with indigo in all the tribes.

F. M. Savina, *Histoire des Miao* (History of the Miao)

A track winds through the heights above the Mong La River. Along it move young girls heading for the fields, their baskets on their backs, water buffalo being herded towards their pasture, hunters armed with crossbows, their prey dangling from their belts, trotting ponies, a Minsk motorcycle loaded with an entire family on the way to Sa Pa. In the distance, huge clumps of bamboo form vertical lines on the wide platform of the rice terraces, which reflect the sunlight or the passing clouds. A Hmong man wearing an indigo cap stands in the river and casts his weighted fishing net into the rapids. The suspension bridge that spans the river sways and then stops. Further away, on the hillside, a Hmong village welcomes tourists. The thatched houses are still made of wooden planks, but it is said that the shaman has gone away.

LEFT
Terraced paddy fields in the Mong La river valley, near Sa Pa.
RIGHT
A Flowered Hmong woman with her children at a tea-stall in Bac Ha.

IMPERIAL ARCHITECTURE

On the green hills that line the banks of the Perfume River, upstream from Huê, the royal tombs of the Nguyên Dynasty stand as monuments in the landscape and in history. Built far from the imperial city that has been destroyed so many times, they were spared the ravages of war. The tombs, surrounded by tall pine trees, are dedicated to the memory of the country's illustrious rulers: Gia Long, Minh Mang, Khai Dinh, Thiêu Tri, Dông Khanh, Tu Duc. For posterity, each of them ordered the construction of a funerary complex, with elaborate tombs covered in sacred symbols.

The monuments fit beautifully into the landscape, each incorporating the vital elements of vegetation, water courses and hills into its structure. Bringing together harmony and aesthetics, an ordered parade of porticos, terraces, canals, basins, temples and pavilions lead up to the tomb itself.

The imperial geomancers and astrologers worked hard to achieve this picturesque merging with the landscape, combining architectural considerations with mystical knowledge. They embarked on a quest for an ideal site, which they called the Blue Dragon, whose air is benevolent, seeking at all costs to avoid the White Tiger with its evil breath. The site and its orientation were determined by *phong thuy*, the Vietnamese version of *feng shui*, the ancient Chinese principles which have been consulted for centuries in Hanoi and Huê.

The entrance to the tombs is through one of two side gates: the monumental gateway to the tomb of Minh Mang was only opened once for the sovereign's body to pass through it and then closed forever. To reach the pavilions, you must cross a wide courtyard filled with two rows of grey sandstone statues of mandarins, ministers, noblemen, brave generals and royal elephants standing as straight and tall as tree-trunks.

Lakes, canals and ornamental ponds in symbolic shapes are covered in pink and white lotus flowers, the Buddhist symbol of purity. Beyond the monumental gateway to the king's tomb lies a row of pavilions designed to the sovereign's specifications. The emperor Minh Mang had them

> **Only religious and imperial buildings were permitted to have stone walls"**

built in increasing order of size, moving from the form of a square (symbol of the earth) through shapes that grow increasingly circular (the symbol of heaven), along an axis that leads from the finite to the infinite.

The pavilions, ornamental ponds, bridges and streams are named after natural features or the virtues that are venerated in Buddhist symbolism: the Bridges of Intelligence and Justice, the Lakes of Pure Clarity, Filial Piety, the Gilded or Divine Phoenix, the Dragon's Beneficence, the Temple of the Venerated Deeds, the Temple of Modesty, and the Temple of the Brilliant Perfection.

By decree, only certain religious and imperial buildings were permitted to have stone walls. The main feature of Vietnamese houses was the wooden frame, made of lim (ironwood). The whole framework was assembled without nails, using mortice and tenon joints, which made it possible to move many of the temples and pavilions. The weight of the structure gave the buildings their firm anchorage to the ground and resistance to typhoons. In Hoi An, some of the wooden rafters combine Vietnamese, Chinese and Japanese influences with grace and originality.

As with their spiritual beliefs, the Vietnamese have maintained their own traditions in architecture while letting in outside influences, which are then adapted to fit their laws and tastes. These combinations can be seen in many palaces and houses, with the combination of colonial Chinese influences resulting in a lively, elegant and dynamic style.

The originality of this architecture is in the way it merges into the visual landscape. It seems bound to respect what is already there, to make it a more beautiful and pleasant place to live in. The plans of the architects and those who commissioned their work were both humble and ambitious: they wanted to combine symbolic, naturalistic, Buddhist and Confucian influences to create an ideal of harmony and poetry.

144

The seven-storey tower of the Thiên Mu Pagoda rises above the Perfume River. According to legend, this is where the figure of a woman appeared to the Lord Nguyên Hoang as he walked to Thuan Hoa: the name Thiên Mu means 'Heavenly Lady'. Where the portico stood, there are now four pillars: the three spaces between them symbolizing three central concepts of Buddhism – emptiness, impermanence and enlightenment. Pagodas are usually built on hills or mounds.

PRECEDING PAGES
Huê: Phuoc Duyên Tower and the pillars of Thiên Mu, the Pagoda of the Heavenly Lady.
LEFT
Huê: the bridge-house of Thanh Toan; the roof of the wooden structure that spans the river is covered in the glazed, semi-cylindrical tiles that are a feature of the Annam region.
RIGHT
The Noon Gate, entrance to the imperial city of Huê, topped by the Pavilion of Five Phoenixes. The tiled roofs are ornamented with dragons and bats.

The frangipani flowers fell from the trees,
spreading the scent of lilies. I remember the large sandy
courtyards, the stagnant ponds covered in waterlilies.
But above all I retain the vision of that darkened room
that I entered without knowing anything, the gravity of
which stopped me on the threshold. I was in the
House of the Soul, the Temple of the Tablet,
the Palace of the Good Deeds of the Spirits.

Roland Dorgelès, *On the Mandarin Road*

The imperial tombs of Huê consist of several buildings. A crescent-shaped pond protects the entrance. Further on, a terrace was built for the celebration of rituals on feast days. The temple dedicated to ancestor worship stands next in line, followed by a pavilion containing a stele on which are engraved the most important events of the reign. Other buildings have been erected as memorials to ancestors and to house the emperor's wives after his death. The royal tomb contains the mortal remains of the sovereign. It is often housed in a circular chamber, symbolizing the sun.

LEFT
Huê: detail of a pavilion containing an effigy of the emperor Minh Mang. •
Huê: tomb of the emperor Khai Dinh.
RIGHT
Portrait of Khai Dinh in his mausoleum.

In the early fifteenth century, Lê Loi was proclaimed king. He embarked on a huge reform of the government of his kingdom of *Dai Viêt*, meaning 'Great Viet'. In a desire to encourage education, he founded the College of the Sons of the State which was open to the sons of mandarins and to the most gifted students from among the ordinary people. If they passed the imperial examinations, they could become mandarins, valuable administrators in the service of the state, under the watchful eye of the sovereign.

LEFT
Ho Chi Minh City: Chinese lantern and gilded stele beneath the beams of Thiên Hau Pagoda in Cholon.
RIGHT
Two senior bureaucrats from the province of Annam. • Huê: interior of the pavilion of the stele of the tomb of Minh Mang. • Rattan furniture on a rickshaw in front of the Noon Gate in Huê. • Hoi An: the wooden doors of a house.
INSET
A carved wooden seal consisting of the repeated character for good luck, surrounded by phoenixes and topped with the yin and yang symbol. • Returning from the Nam Giao Festival through the Noon Gate in the imperial city of Huê. • A young emperor of Annam.

152

The ancient plans of the imperial city show all of the pavilions erected within the sacred complex surrounding the palace of he whom it was forbidden to name: the Elect, the Representative of Heaven. Each pavilion had a function, and there were strict rules as to who was allowed access and who was forbidden to enter according to rank, title and gender. The names of these pavilions are evocative of palace life at the time: the Gate of Virtue, the Palace of the Queen Mother, the King's Library, the Pavilion of the Scholars, the Palace of Examinations, the Theatre Royal, the King's Wardrobe, Barracks of the King's Bearers, Reception Pavilion, the Barracks of the Magnificent. As in other royal courts, women and concubines, eunuchs, guards and members of the divine family were housed in pavilions attached to that of the sovereign, so as to be ready at all times to serve their sovereign.

LEFT
The imperial city of Huê: Thai Hoa Palace.
RIGHT
A board game in a pagoda in Hoi An.

The storm has melted, thrones change hands,
Leaves in the wind, they do not know where to land.
From the top of the palace, they have dropped into the deep.
The clasp and the vase break, fragile is their destiny.
Where is the dance of the court and the rituals of yesteryear?
Their eyelids are closed, their remains are uncollected.
Alas! No incense burns in their memory.

Nguyên Du, *Mille Ans de littérature viétnamienne*
(A Thousand Years of Vietnamese Literature)

RIGHT
The Imperial City of Huê: the
Pavilion of the Glorious Coming
(Hiên Lâm) is the only three-storey
building in the complex.

In the Temple of Literature in Hanoi, on each side of the Basin of Celestial Clarity, eighty-two steles honour those who passed the imperial examinations held in Thanh Long (now known as Hanoi) between the fifteenth and eighteenth centuries.
On Sundays, the young descendants of these illustrious servants of the state would come to prostrate themselves before the stele on which the name of their ancestor appeared.

PRECEDING PAGES
Huê: the palatial tomb of Tu Duc, fourth king of the Nguyên Dynasty. As a lover of literature, he would come to the poetry pavilion to read and compose odes beside the waters of Lake Luu Khiêm.
LEFT
Huê: statue of a general on the terrace of the tomb of Minh Mang. • Hanoi: detail of the portico of the One-Pillar Pagoda. • Huê: statues of the royal elephants in the shade of the frangipani trees outside the tomb of Minh Mang.
RIGHT
Hanoi: the Temple of Literature, dedicated to Confucius; the central avenue leads to the gate of the Constellation of Literature. • Decorative terracotta tiles in the Temple of Literature. • Wild ginger flower.

At the beautiful garden house of Lac Tinh Viên, Mrs Khanh Nam greets visitors. In the drawing room, this royal descendant stands tall and erect and uses formal codes of greeting: her head bowed, a delicate smile on her lips, her hands clasped. She is hospitable and full of respect, speaking on behalf of her family, never using the first person singular, and mentioning her ancestor not by his name but by his title. Out of deference, she uses a high-pitched voice and a vocabulary that is designed never to offend. In the architectural setting of this house that once belonged to a mandarin, her presence is a reminder of the rich culture of the city formerly known as Phu Xuan (now Huê) and of the ideals that were venerated by her honoured ancestor Hong Khang, tenth son of the Emperor Minh Mang.

LEFT
Huê: a corridor in the garden house of Lac Tinh Viên.
RIGHT
The drawing room, decorated with a portrait of the house's former master.

CITY LIFE

Old maps of Vietnam show very few towns. The country was very rural, the thousands of villages scattered over the low-lying plains of the north, in the Red River valley and delta. Towards the south, the landscape broadens out, dotted with settlements along the coast, right down to the Mekong Delta. Some villages were grouped around a citadel, which served as an administrative, civil and military centre, and these settlements grew into the provincial capitals. True towns and cities did not emerge until the nineteenth century. The layout of these cities had a pragmatic reasoning behind it, taking account of roads and navigable waterways, geography and exposure to the elements (rain, wind, typhoons), and risks of enemy incursions.

In antiquity, peasants and merchants would come and sell their wares beside the city walls. Today, a new industrial belt, a mixture of light and heavy industry, provides work for the city dwellers, who are still fed by the crops grown in the surrounding countryside. Since economic expansion, the urban areas have been transformed and modernized, growing denser and expanding like multi-headed hydras into the surrounding land. In the city centres, skyscrapers have been built whose tops are shrouded in the huge monsoon clouds. The outskirts are home to those who have been displaced from the centre of town by redevelopment, along with the latest arrivals, thousands of rootless young people in search of work and a better quality of life.

In its early years, Thanh Long (now known as Hanoi) was a fortress surrounded by a group of villages. Specialist markets were held there: a grapefruit market, a coconut palm market, a rice market, a fish market and a frog market. Trade has continued and the complex of markets is now known as the Old Quarter or the 36 Guilds District, after the trade guilds that were once based here. The streets take their names from the trades of that period: Veil Street, Raft Street, Brine Street, Sugar and Salt Street, Mat Street, Tinplate Street, Fan Street and Medicine Street, Silk Street, Brocade Street, Paper Street, Bamboo Street and Hemp Street. In the years that followed, the unruly river and lakes were tamed by embankments and many temples were built, the strong walls of the fortress vanishing in a maze of narrow streets.

Yellow ochre, dark green and jade: the colours of the walls and shutters in Hanoi are striking features of an architecture which has successfully combined oriental and Western styles. There is no feverish building here; everything is measured, meted out sparingly, except for the sound of car horns. But despite the lack of space in the cramped flats, city life cannot be confined. People enjoy taking chairs outdoors to sit on the pavement. The street itself also overflows into the houses. You can hear the cries of the soup-sellers, the shouts of the children in the nearby school yard. On the pavement, you can find manicurists and hairdressers, knife-grinders, women selling ice-creams and sweets, and a host of traders displaying their wares on the doorstep.

Ho Chi Minh City, the megalopolis of the south, is a daughter of the tropics. Fuelled by the trade in the Mekong Delta, the focus of hope and envy, it has had difficulty controlling its own growth. Work is still being done: containing and cleaning the backwaters, draining the swamps that enclosed and once separated the towns of Saigon, Gia Dinh and Cholon (the Chinese district), which have now been reunited administratively into Ho Chi Minh City. Renovations are happening, tower blocks are springing up. The former Saigon is looking to the sky, towards the outside world, towards its future.

Here the keys to happiness are simple: a motor scooter, a mobile phone, a gang of friends. At mealtimes, phones ring constantly, suggestions and invitations flying like bullets: a game of billiards, a soup stand, some *banh xeo* pancakes and spring rolls, a fashionable café, a beer with grilled squid, and the finest *trê* (a sugary dessert). This concentration of people brings a hunger for community and identity in which anything and everything can become an excuse for a gathering, for spending time together and sharing a few moments of life. On Saturday evening, the endless dance of motor scooters begins, going for a spin around the cathedral, down Dong Khoi Street to the Saigon River and then riding up Lê Loi Boulevard. People chat to each other from their bikes, by the light of their headlamps, yelling and gossiping, sending each other burning looks and meaningful smiles. This young city is changing, but in many ways it remains the same. It is this love of hedonistic freedom, combined with a longing to embrace others, that gives Ho Chi Minh City its special charm.

Darkness falls at six o'clock in the evening throughout the year in the tropics. In Hanoi and Ho Chi Minh City, boys and girls all take to two wheels in a human tide, handlebar to handlebar, causing massive traffic jams. The city throbs with the sounds of karaoke, mobile phones and the roaring engines of the motor scooters. Those without wheels often pair off into couples to sip lemonade in a café or eat ice cream. Others quench their thirst for company on the Internet, appeasing their curiosity about the wider world. Online chat has revolutionized romantic encounters, and it is perfectly suited to the shyness and inhibitions of these young people and their playful struggles against parental restrictions, which are still fairly strong.

PRECEDING PAGES
The business district of Ho Chi Minh City.
LEFT
Hanoi: a nightclub entrance in Trang Thi Street.
RIGHT
Ho Chi Minh City. Every Saturday night, young people get on their motor scooters and fill the streets. • Hanoi: backstage at a fashion show, girls cluster around a mobile phone game.

Throughout Vietnam, the youthfulness of the population is impossible to ignore. Along the crowded pavements and in the tightly packed schoolyards, the energy and dynamism of Vietnamese young people is everywhere. Half the population is aged under twenty and has never experienced the horrors of war. The new generation is seeking its own identity and testing out its own limits in a world that was unknown to its parents, a world of computer games, sports fields and shopping malls.

LEFT
North Vietnam, Phat Diêm: young girls wearing the *ao dai*, the Vietnamese national costume. • Diên Biên Phu: chatting and playing online games in a cybercafé. • Soccer practice in Huê. • Schoolchildren sit cross-legged in a schoolyard in Tran Quoc Toan, Hanoi.
RIGHT
Newly qualified primary school teachers outside their classroom.

In Ho Chi Minh City, life is lived in the *hems*. These narrow backstreets are a winding maze of alleyways, hard to follow logically but always full of surprises. The houses are painted in a multitude of candy colours: mint green, sky blue, strawberry pink and lemon yellow. The houses are too cramped to comfortably contain the large families, so the children are forced to play outdoors, giving the streets the liveliness of a playground. Gurgling babies are promenaded in their pushchairs; grandfathers take the air in their pyjamas; little boys chase balls and little girls jump as high as the sky over elastic skipping ropes.

LEFT
Ho Chi Minh City: playing in a *hem*, an alleyway in Cholon.
RIGHT
Ho Chi Minh City: behind a stall in Tan Dinh market.

174

To the sensation-seeking demands of young people, society responds by offering Hollywood-style global culture. Their parents, who lived through the interminable war years, were forced to lead more sheltered lives. But curiously, rebellion is now being seen as a normal thing. The Cai Luong open-air theatre is out of date; people want to see preview showings of the latest movies that they've read about on the Internet. Young people in Vietnam are looking to the West and don't want to be left behind. On television, hugely popular South Korean and Thai soap operas offer a taste of modernity, consumerism and luxury, something for everyone to aspire to. The young believe that they should have access to the same movies, TV shows and concerts as other Asian countries or the West: in this globalized world, it seems only fair, after all.

LEFT
The business centre of Ho Chi Minh City.
RIGHT
Ho Chi Minh City: a film poster outside the Galaxy multiplex cinema.

In the cities, street food is available almost everywhere in the streets and markets. In Hanoi, the food stalls are called *com bui*, 'dust restaurants'. From the pavements, they offer a selection of local dishes on tiny plates. You just point at what you want, and create your own combination of foods and flavours: spring rolls with fragrant herbs, bamboo shoots with grilled meat, stir-fried meat and sautéed water spinach. In Ho Chi Minh City, travelling food-sellers and tiny local restaurants offer all kinds of soups. Everyone has their own favourite, depending on their mood, the occasion and the time of day. There is something for every taste: a light *miên* with cellophane noodles in a meat and vegetable broth, *hu tiêu* with its Cambodian flavours, nourishing *chau* based on ground rice, the famous *pho* containing thin strips of beef or chicken with thick, flat noodles, and not forgetting Chinese medicinal soup with ginseng.

LEFT
Ho Chi Minh City: a soup-vendor's barrow in Tan Dinh market.
RIGHT
Ho Chi Minh City: the Metropolitan Building facing the cathedral in Paris Square.

I wander down an alley in which only Buddhist artefacts are sold. The traders are less insistent than in Saigon; here they do not sing the praises of their goods. ...This walk has made me thirsty and I stop at a little stall and buy a coconut which the seller deftly splits open with a machete, enabling me to drink the contents through a straw.... One does not see old French cars as in Saigon, no Citroën engines, no ancient European buses. The trucks that clatter past are of Russian or Chinese manufacture, the few new cars are imported from Japan. Ahead of me, women are busy setting out stools and a table on the pavement. At midday, they will be opening a temporary restaurant.

Carolijn Visser, *Voices and Visions: A Journey Through Vietnam Today*

In the streets of the big cities, fashion changes fast. Once upon a time, when Confucian tradition dominated, women would wear a simple bodice under a fairly loose traditional tunic, which revealed little of the figure. Then came the *ao dai*, a traditional costume that was more close-fitting. The collar hugs the neck and the tunic, with its tailored sleeves, has front and back panels that fall over wide trousers. Young girls have new costumes made for special occasions or when they find an attractive new fabric. Worn casually by elegant young girls who ride by on their bicycles, a well-cut *ao dai* on an attractive figure could turn the head of the most jaded spirit.

LEFT
Ho Chi Minh City: among the women on the street near the Ben Thanh market, one is wearing an *ao dai*.
RIGHT
Hanoi: in front of a concert venue in the Old Quarter.

From north to south, the towns are expanding quickly. In Hanoi, ring roads now encircle the city, and motorbikes, buses, vans and trucks ride endlessly around the capital. In many places, tower blocks and individual homes are rising high above the ground, pushing back the fields and market gardens. Space is already in short supply in the centre of Ho Chi Minh City. Office buildings and apartment blocks jostle for space and the overworked city-planners construct the future like children playing with building blocks. Some buildings stand very tall, others are brightly coloured. At night, from the top of the tower blocks, the lights of the traffic are transformed into a headless dragon winding between the buildings, beside the river and into the nerve centre of the magical city.

LEFT
Hanoi: rush hour in Hai Ba Trung Street.
RIGHT
Ho Chi Minh City: Mê Linh Square in the business district.

A legend was born in Hanoi, in the time of the hero Lê Loi. One day, a golden turtle emerged from the lake to present Lê Loi with a sword. Seeing this as a sign that he had to chase the Minh Chinese invaders out of the country, he took the sword, won the final victory and became king. When he came to thank the lake after his coronation, the golden turtle once again emerged from the waters to take back the sword. The place was therefore named Hoan Kiêm, the Lake of the Recovered Sword.

PRECEDING PAGES
A temple in a narrow street in the Old Quarter of Hanoi.
LEFT
Hanoi: an altar for travellers at Long Biên Station.
RIGHT
Hanoi: the Thê Huc Bridge, the Bridge of the Morning Glow, on its tall red posts, leads to the Ngoc Son Pagoda, on Lake Hoan Kiêm. The Tower of the Paintbrush marks the entrance to the pagoda and is inscribed with the line: 'Write on the blue of the sky.'

At about six thirty, the display windows of the shops
are still padlocked. Only the doors open lazily to allow
the shopworkers to sweep the pavements, the lady owners
to take the air, yawning, their hair in curlers, their clothes
disarranged, open, waiting for the sellers of steamed
wontons, hot sticky rice, sandwiches and pâtés to
provide their husbands' and children's breakfasts.
By seven in the morning, all the shops are open,
sparkling with lights as customers traipse through,
the merchandise impeccably displayed. A space
glowing with colour, vibrant with sound,
in which the dust is beginning to rise.

Duong Thu Huong, *No Man's Land*

The cities of Vietnam have a certain air of chaotic, joyful kitsch about them. They are never dull because they never take themselves too seriously; somehow, they become magnets for well-being and prosperity. Despite the sprawl, the noise, the clutter and the air pollution, these powerhouses of energy and excitement are virtually impossible to resist.

LEFT
Ho Chi Minh City: Suoi Tiên water park. • Football game at sunrise in the city centre. • Household goods for sale in Tan Dinh market. • Magazines on sale at a kiosk. • The city centre.
INSET
View of Silk Street and other narrow streets in old Hanoi in the early twentieth century. • Two posters for popular Vietnamese films.
RIGHT
Ho Chi Minh City: a travelling manicurist offers her services on a customer's doorstep. • Hanoi: a street barber works outside a pagoda in the Old Quarter.

In the 36 Guilds district of Hanoi, the 'tube houses' with their narrow frontages have gradually been replaced or rebuilt. In the place where roofs were formerly not allowed to exceed 'the height of the king on his litter borne on the shoulders of his people', true tower blocks are being constructed. The depth of the plots of land makes it possible to build small hotels: some of the tube houses go back twenty, fifty and up to a hundred metres from the street. The narrow facades still include shopfronts, but the pavements are no longer packed with the goods that were once the speciality of the district. Mats, silk clothing, sugar, rattan, fans, tin pots and pans and traditional medicines gave their names to these streets, but the goods themselves are now being moved away, and sold in small shops in the Old Quarter.

LEFT
Hanoi: Mat Street.
RIGHT
Hanoi: masks and drums on sale in Cholon, ready for the Tết Festival.

THE SOUTH CHINA SEA

From the shores of the Gulf of Tonkin to the mangrove swamps of the low alluvial plains along the Cambodian border, the Vietnamese coastline stretches for more than 2,000 km (1,200 miles), sometimes green from the paddy fields and mangrove trees, sometimes yellow from the dunes of fine sand. In the east and south, it is bordered by two seas whose velvety blue edges wash against these delightful lands.

The eastern seaboard witnessed the arrival of the Chinese and Mongolian fleets of invaders. The southern seaboard saw the arrival of sailing ships from Japan, India, Arabia and Portugal. The voyages of these ships were governed by the prevailing winds; in winter, the Chinese and Japanese sailed down from the north, while the Indian ships and those from Malacca and Batavia came from the south with the summer monsoon. Ports moved or changed their names when they silted up or as a result of historic events: Kaûthara became Nha Trang, Fai Fo became Hoi An; the island port of Vandon, off Quang Yen, is now abandoned.

It was in the tenth century that the land of Great Viêt first gained its independence from China. The Kinh, the majority ethnic group of Vietnam, lived in the north, while the south was occupied by the kingdom of Champa, home to the Cham, a people of Malay and Indonesian descent who have lived there for twelve centuries.

The Vietnamese are wary of the sea, and have long turned their backs on it. Vandon was turned into a trading port for goods from Siam, Java and China, and was designed to prevent foreigners from entering the hinterland and spying on the people. Only the Cham were happy to venture out into the seas around their country. They earned their livelihood from privateering and international trade, exporting ivory and ebony, rhinoceros horns and elephant tusks, swallows' nests and rattan, sugar and silks along the Spice Road.

The ports of Champa were famous and they had some illustrious visitors: mariners with grand designs, merchants and soldiers on the road to fortune and recognition, mystical monks. Marco Polo stopped off here on his way to China. The

The Vietnamese are wary of the sea, and have long turned their backs on it"

legendary Chinese merchant Zheng He used it as his fleet's home port when he sailed towards the Malacca Straits, the Sunda Islands and India. Cham sailors established trading routes with distant Java. It was here in the mid-fifteenth century that King Kertawijaya converted to Islam on the advice of his wife Darawati, a princess of Champa.

In both north and south, the greedy deltas have devoured the land on their way to the sea, altering its shape. These geographical features have given the country its shape and the nickname, ' the balcony of Asia'. The sea, languorous during the dry season, stirs into a fury during the summer monsoons. Typhoons from the Philippines regularly end their journey on the coasts of Vietnam, beating out the last of their strength on the coconut palms of the southern and central regions, tearing off roofs and beaching unlucky vessels caught away from their moorings. The breakers hit the plains, erode the coast, breach and devour the sea defences, rendering useless any human attempts to curb their appetite. Who would have ever believed they could fight the strength of the ocean and build a dam here against the might of the Pacific?

Mankind has long understood that it is vital to compromise with the sea, and adapt to it. Although the briny waters cannot be tamed, they can be enclosed and oxygenated for farming shrimp and catfish; the paddy fields can be protected by high, carefully maintained levees, even though the rains submerge and flood them in the rainy season.

Under the tropical sun, people now take advantage of their holidays to enjoy the pleasures of the beach. They flock noisily to the long sandy strands of Vung Tau (near Ho Chi Minh City) and Do Don (near Haiphong), dressed to the nines and intending to enjoy the fresh air, the waves and a few days of leisure. The days draw to a close amid the scent of grilled fish and seafood and the sounds of shouting children and teams of teenagers playing ball on the beach. In the evening, the crowds relax in the seaside cafés to the sound of karaoke, celebrating the advent of the leisure society.

Along its 2,000 km (1,200 miles) of coastline, the whole of the Vietnamese seaboard is exposed to the rising sun. The Vietnamese geographers of the ancient kingdoms that became Annam and Tonkin called this sea, which faces eastward towards the Philippines, the 'Eastern Sea'. South of the 17th parallel, sailors named the territorial waters off Cochin-China the 'South Sea', the waters that separated the continent from the Malayan and Indonesian archipelago. Both of these are now considered part of the South China Sea.

PRECEDING PAGES
Sampans moored in a bay near Huê.
LEFT
South Vietnam: the fishing port of Vung Tau, 120 kilometres (75 miles) from Ho Chi Minh City.
RIGHT
Annam: paddling in a woven boat at Tourane (now known as Da Nang), 1907.

Though they have never truly specialized in seafaring, the Vietnamese have developed a variety of ocean-going craft, which combine foreign influences with local adaptations. The junks used in the Gulf of Tonkin were built in the Chinese style; their sails were made from cotton or woven bamboo. In the Thanh Hoa region, sailors used rafts made of thick bamboo stalks lashed together; these were very stable, and when moored, they were able to withstand the many typhoons that ravage the central region every year. The sampans of the south, with their rice-straw sails, use construction techniques borrowed from Malay boats.

LEFT
Annam: boats returning from deep-sea fishing on the beach at Qui Nhon. •
Fish-farming in the Bay of Lang Co, in central Vietnam.

RIGHT
Fishermen drawing in their nets at Qui Nhon, Annam, c. 1900. • Drying fish at Nha Trang. • Fish market in Hoi An. • Traditional woodcut of a fish.

INSET
Annam: sampans sailing in the Bay of Tourane (now Da Nang) in the early twentieth century. • Stamps showing three types of wooden boat.

Nuoc mam is a fermented fish liquor concentrate manufactured by the Vietnamese. There are vintages, as for wine, that of Phu Quoc being the finest. It smells strongly, it is true, but it is delicious. It is used to flavour all types of food, even meat. In the hospital, I used to give a tablespoon of it every morning to my convalescents. I had a sample of it analyzed by a laboratory; it contains everything that the body needs: salts, calcium, iron, phosphorus, vitamins, etc. I used to think that with rice and nuoc mam, and a little opium for treatment, one could take a trip around the world – I still think so.

Pierre Schoendoerffer, *The Paths of the Sea*

RIGHT
A fine catch for sale in the
fish market at Hoi An.

At dawn, the wide bay of Nha Trang blazes with colour. Old ladies come to meditate on the beach, seated in the lotus position, their faces caressed by the sea breezes. The serene wrinkles of their faces are mirrored in the gentle waves, and their open hands reflect the reddish glow of the rising sun. The long fronds of the coconut palms seem to gently comb the air, while a few bathers enjoy the breaking waves.

LEFT AND RIGHT
Nha Trang: the view from the beach.

Sea-bathing is not a longstanding tradition in South Vietnam. The currents that run parallel to the shoreline are powerful and can carry away swimmers, sometimes right out to sea. Some children stay at the edge of the beach, while others use old inner tubes to keep them afloat. Out at sea, the huge container ships sail ceaselessly to and fro, evidence of the region's booming economy.

LEFT
On the beach, the fishermen's wives sort the small fry. • Evening falls on the beach at Long Ai. • Sunday morning on the beach at Vung Tau, 120 km (75 miles) from Ho Chi Minh City. • Every morning at Vung Tau, the boats are hauled up the beach. • A runner passes behind a stall selling cooked fish. • A food-seller offers hard-boiled eggs and dried squid from her yoke.

RIGHT
Nha Trang: a family relaxing on the beach. • At Vung Tau, children's names are written on the inner tubes that can be rented out for use in the water.

The recent trade boom has enabled the emergence of a newly affluent middle class. They can now be found at the tourist attractions and on the beaches, in family groups or with friends. They timidly paddle in the water or sit among the gentle waves, almost as if they did not dare to fully profit from their richly deserved leisure time. Perhaps this is because Vietnamese society has long been imprinted with a belief that work is of fundamental importance. While they teach their children to swim, parents themselves are learning how to enjoy a new style of living.

LEFT
Holidaymakers on the beach.
RIGHT
Family bathing in the Bay of Vung Tau.

A WORLD INSIDE

Hanoi, the present day. Three pairs of shoes on the doorstep of a house. A tray resting on the table, tiny cups and the wafting scent of green tea. A cup is extended to the guest, held in clasped hands accompanied by a small smile. This is how strangers are welcomed into a Vietnamese home. The tea is not merely a drink, it is a rite of passage. It honours visitors who enter even the humblest home, acting as an invitation to come inside a coded and compartmentalized but accessible world, that of the interior, of the intimate. Once the cup has been put down, a magical key seems to turn, and you are suddenly less of a stranger, your existence recognized and accepted by the family. In Vietnam, the concept of home (*nha*) is often extolled. This word is used to mean the house, the spouse and the family, the central unit that structures life in Vietnamese society.

The space into which you are received as a visitor is the equivalent of the living room, sometimes even the only room. Once the ice has been broken, this space becomes yours in some small way. As you sit cross-legged on the straw mat, the children timidly approach to watch you, then gradually start to cling to you. Within this small space, rice and sleep, silence and laughter are shared. In a corner stands an altar to the family ancestors. Every day, offerings are placed there in front of photographs of the deceased: a bunch of lilies, some oranges, incense or rice wine, depending on the tastes of the person in question.

Huê, in the late nineteenth century. During the reign of the Emperor Thanh Thai, a modest but illustrious man came to live beside the Phu Cam canal. He chose three characters, three words to name his garden home: Lac, 'happy'; Tinh, 'calm'; Viên, 'garden'. Not far from the citadel in which he worked as a mandarin, he lived in peace. Wife, children, nephews, cousins, a large and extended family shared the space and the restrained yet charming buildings, surrounded by shady open passageways.

Once through the door of Lac Tinh Viên, visitors are confronted with an openwork screen topped by divinities, inviting their gaze to wander right and left through the garden plants. While the areca palm points its leaves to the sky, the betel climbs and winds around a pole and fans out its dark green

" Three pairs of shoes
on the doorstep of a house..."

leaves. Along the colonnades, climbing plants delicately stretch themselves, sowing splashes of scented colour here and there.

Behind the screen wall, three buildings are arranged in a U-shape around an open pavilion standing on four ironwood columns. The family tablets do not reveal the name of the practitioner of *phong thuy* who planned these buildings so carefully. Nothing has been left to chance: orientation with the heavens, the distribution of masses and spaces according to secret rules, the circulation of liquids, winds and spirits.

At the heart of the central building lies the altar of the ancestors. Behind a bamboo curtain, there are tablets engraved in *chu nom* (an old Vietnamese script based on Chinese characters), recording the lineage. Offerings and small statues of the Buddha in lacquered or gilded wood are displayed on neighbouring altars.

The living and working spaces are laid out on either side of the altars. On the left is the reception room in which tea is served. The master's office, sober and even ascetic, leads off it; he gave this pavilion the name of Van Trai, 'house of

questioning'. It is here that, on his retirement, he became a tutor for all the children in the family.

The central pavilion in the courtyard has no walls. Prominently displayed on a wide rectangular frame are two engraved gilded characters representing the word 'humanity'. It is here that His Excellency Hong Khang gathered his children every week so that they could witness their father giving alms to beggars. Teaching without words and by example has marked the generations who have lived in this space. And, in Kim Ngoc's domain, in the pine forest near the Perfume River, people still think of him and remember him. On the altar of his burial mound, incense is burned on the anniversary of his death and the devoted Lan, his descendant, regularly talks about him and revives his memory. Beyond the wars and the long years, all those who lived at Lac Tinh Viên still remember the civilized garden house of the Prince.

In communal homes,
pagodas and community
temples, the entrance leads
into the main axis of the
building, letting the spirits
circulate freely. The threshold
is a filter that separates the
outside world from the
spiritual space within; the
faithful are asked to leave their
bicycles, hats and sandals
there. The heavy roof beams
of religious buildings are
supported by strong ironwood
pillars, with high and wide
spaces between. The main
prayer rooms are welcoming
and reassuring, its air of
serenity giving worshippers
the peace needed to meditate
and calm their inner selves.

PRECEDING PAGES
Ho Chi Minh City: entrance to a pagoda
in Cholon, the Chinese district.
LEFT
Hanoi: the entrance of the pagoda
adjoining the One-Pillar Pagoda.
RIGHT
Hanoi: porch of a pagoda near the
Western Lake.

And then, to impress my imagination,
inside the modest dwelling of my friend from Assam,
there was an altar to the ancestors that was always
decorated: joss sticks, fruits laid out as an offering,
red and gold images of the spirits with eyes made up like
actors in a theatre. By some obscure association of ideas,
this worship reminded me of the red tom-tom
on the Island of the Ogre.

Philippe Franchini, *Continental Saigon*

Houses and apartments are cramped in the cities of Vietnam. Every available space is in use and the large size of families means that people live on top of each other. Indoors, there is often no such thing as privacy. Everyone's living space inevitably encroaches on that of others. Karaoke music, the sounds from the television, conversations – there's a cacophony of noise, and it's hard to escape the din for a moment of peace. Yet no one seems to complain about the cramped conditions, with the exception of young couples who sometimes have to share a limited space with their parents, separated merely by a thin curtain.

LEFT
Hanoi: extra coaching in the home of a primary school teacher.
RIGHT
A student's room in the suburbs of Ho Chi Minh City.

Interiors are designed according to the principles of phong thuy (feng shui), which takes into account the influences of the earth and the laws of nature. Everything must be done so that air and water circulate in the most auspicious way, bringing positive energy into the household. A bed goes in one place, its head against the wall; a table goes in another. Windows match the points of the compass, and a ceremony is performed before moving into the property. These conditions ensure that family harmony will be maintained.

LEFT
Café in a small street in Ho Chi Minh City. • Father and son in a 'tube house' in Ho Chi Minh City. • Restaurant serving pho (noodle soup) in a house in Hanoi. • Drying chopsticks in an inner courtyard in Hanoi. • A colonial-era interior in Ho Chi Minh City.
INSET
Dining room of a house in Saigon, c. 1914. • The two favourites of the King of Annam, early twentieth century. • A tam cuc card, a traditional card game played in North Vietnam. • Yin and yang seals.
RIGHT
North Vietnam: Catholic worshippers gather before high mass at the Phat Diêm cathedral. • Woodcut showing the streets of old Hanoi.

There was one big room on the landing, and a whole family sat and lay about in it with the effect of a camp which might be struck at any moment. Small teacups stood about everywhere, and there were lots of cardboard boxes full of unidentifiable objects and fibre suitcases already strapped; there was an old lady sitting on a big bed, two boys and two girls, a baby crawling on the floor, three middle-aged women in old brown peasant trousers and jackets, and two old men in a corner in blue silk mandarin coats, playing mahjong – they paid no attention to my coming, they played rapidly, identifying each piece by touch, and the noise was like shingle turning on a beach after a wave withdraws.

Graham Greene, *The Quiet American*

The chronicles of the province of Thai Binh record a ritual that was performed at festivals in villages which honoured a thief, the lustful or a tiger as their patron spirits. The Turning Out of the Lanterns was held on the sixth and seventh days of the first lunar month, in honour of the thief spirit. On the last night of the festival, all of the lanterns were extinguished at the same time, and it was traditional for people to reach out and touch in the dark, pouncing on their neighbours or trying to steal a kiss from passing girls. It was certainly no place for prudish souls.

PRECEDING PAGES
On Sunday, these inhabitants of Cholon turn their living room into a motorbike garage.
LEFT
A lantern-maker's shop, c. 1907.
RIGHT
Paper lanterns being made in Cholon.

In the traditional medicine stores of Cholon (the Chinese district of Ho Chi Minh City), patients come to consult a doctor. The man in the white tunic takes the pulse of customers sitting by the entrance. Depending on the case, he may also examine the whites of their eyes as well as the colour and condition of the tongue. Then he writes out a prescription which the patient hands in at the cashier's desk. A herbalist unfolds papers on the counter and fills the prescription. Peel, bark, dried flowers and fruit, fungi, bulbs and roots, all of the ingredients listed are taken from the wooden drawers that cover the wall, then mixed and weighed. All that remains is to wait for the cashier to tot up the bill on her abacus and pay the money. Many Vietnamese still put their faith in this traditional style of medicine.

LEFT
In the Cholon fish market.
RIGHT
Interior of a traditional pharmacy in Cholon.

234

'With or without sugar? Iced or hot? With or without condensed milk?' she asks. Coffee is first strained through an aluminium filter, then poured out for the customers seated on little chairs at the edge of the pavement. Miss Linh watches them as they drink. The awning, consisting of a patchwork of cloths and scarves, filters the light that pours down onto the heads of the two men, giving one of them crimson hair, and the other a polished bald head of buttercup yellow. Sitting beside the coffee-grinder, Linh inhales the acrid, sweet smell of the beans and reminisces about the high plateaux, her childhood in Buôn Me Thuôt, the life she lived before she came to Ho Chi Minh City.

LEFT
Ho Chi Minh City: a shop selling all kinds of bric-a-brac.
RIGHT
Ho Chi Minh City: an improvised pavement restaurant.

236

In her couture workshop, the stylist is busy preparing for the latest stream of customers. Tunics are altered to fit the slim bodies of the models; amber silk satin flatters the skin and makes complexions glow. Today she produces fashionable figure-hugging cuts, highlighting the body's curves or draping fabric to show off a low-cut back. Nonetheless, a certain degree of modesty is always maintained.

LEFT
A village seamstress in the Hanoi countryside. • Embroidery lessons in a training centre in Ba Ria. • A dressmaker in Ho Chi Minh City. • Fabrics for sale at the market in Cholon. • Preparing for a runway show in Minh Hanh's fashion studio. • A Minh Hanh fashion show at the Temple of Literature in Hanoi
RIGHT
Ho Chi Minh City: a dress shop in Hai Ba Trung street. • Girls wearing the *ao dai* in Phat Diêm.

It is said that in the nineteenth century, when a boy was six years old and attended school for the first time, he would present his teacher with a cockerel which would be sacrificed on the altar to Confucius. Lessons were taught in the homes of the nobility, in schools or in pagodas. Classical texts were studied, including the *Book of Filial Piety* and the *Three Character Classic*, which had been standards for hundreds of years. At the age of fifteen, depending on the examination results, a pupil could enter the triennial competitive examinations, marking the start of the 'Great Learning'. Poetry, the *Classic of Rites*, the *Book of Changes*, philosophy, rhetoric and history were among the topics studied. Between the ages of twenty-five and forty-five, when the student's knowledge was considered to be sufficient, he would be permitted to enter the imperial examinations, in the hope of joining the state bureaucracy as a mandarin.

LEFT
Vinh Long: girls studying at the high school where the mother of the writer Marguerite Duras was once a teacher.
RIGHT
Interior of a classroom in the mid-twentieth century.

ALONG THE RIVERS

The great rivers flow down from the foothills of the Himalayas, pouring and winding through the deep gorges that they have forged, turning into rapids between the high mountains of the Annamite range. Swollen by the heavy rains, they descend to the plains where they slow to a lazy speed, spreading out in their broad beds, through the rice terraces edged with clumps of giant bamboo. The heavy load of silt is borne along, the colour of ochre and burnt sienna. As the rivers approach the deltas, the waters lose their strength and run out of power. Attacked by the tides, their course reverses, the coastal waters pushing deep inland, capsizing craft twice a day, as if they were children's toys.

The rivers mirror the country's history. Each has its own story; the chronicle of Vietnam is imprinted along the courses of the great rivers. The Red River basin does not merely contain a waterway; it is the cradle of a whole civilization.

Originally, all the towns and cities depended on the network of waterways, for trade, protection of strategic defence in wartime. Some of the names of these towns and cities are intimately connected with their rivers. One example is Ha Tiên, which means 'river dwelling of the fairies'.

Some rivers have been given human names, or perhaps the opposite is the case, and the daughters and sons of the sampan-owners have taken the names of rivers. Thanh Ha (Clear River), Truong Giang (Long River): these magical syllables recall poetic and sensual images of the waters glistening like mirrors, gentle as warm breath. Small streams, waterfalls or mountain rapids, narrow rivers, slow-moving powerful waterways, a tangle of backwaters between the palms and mangroves: there is water everywhere. It filters between the chequerboards of the paddy fields, a lifeline in the Vietnamese countryside. All these rivers flow east towards the sea, their speed changing with the seasons.

" The waters glistening like mirrors,
gentle as warm breath..."

On the canals and rivers, life stretches out onto the waters. In the backwaters of the Mekong Delta, the floating markets arrive and set up their stalls with the first light of day, selling fruits, vegetables, noodle soup, groceries, rice cakes or breads, fish and crabs. The women even come to do their shopping in rowing boats. Beneath a modest iron bridge that spans a tributary of the river, water buffalo wallow in the muddy shallows. Mischievous children are perched on their backs, pretending to race each other; clutching the huge horns of these gentle beasts like handlebars, they lean over dangerously as they negotiate imaginary bends.

On the high plains, the creaking and squeaking of the waterwheels can still be heard, the water rising from terrace to terrace with each turn. On the quiet embankments that surround and overlook the rivers, cows and water buffalo graze peacefully, watching the passing convoys of barges laden with sand, coal or sacks of rice.

When evening falls on the Perfume River, the sampans huddle together into improvised villages that expand and contract, coming and going as the hours pass by, according to the tasks each person has to perform. A fisherman mends his net, a young girl prepares water spinach for dinner, a tangle of children giggle and play. The fragrant scent of cooking rice rises from the sampans as their owners prepare for the night.

246

In this land of a thousand rivers, life requires some compromise with the waters. It has always been necessary to tame them, contain them, and cross them by any means available. Whether they are old friends or yesterday's enemies, rivers have been forced to become allies, although watchfulness is still necessary. Many villages are close to waterways and everyday life is lived on the river banks. The children gather to bathe; the duck-keepers guard their flocks; the water buffalo cool themselves in the shallows between the clumps of bamboo, letting the water drip from their long horns that point skywards, as if in homage to the heavens.

PRECEDING PAGES
North Vietnam: fishermen on the Ky Cung River, near the Chinese border at Lang Son.
LEFT
North Vietnam: duck-herder on the Hoang Long River, near Hoa Lu.
RIGHT
North Vietnam, Lang Son province, a group of water buffalo by the river.

We find ourselves on the Bassac, a branch of the Mekong. The river is as wide as a lake. We pass in front of a large island, flat and green and level with the water. Gradually, everything fades into delicate greys. A breeze rises, bringing a little coolness. This is the arroyo at half past five, with pewter-coloured reflections between the still trees. In an inlet, water buffalo are bathing. Their bodies cannot be seen. Only their heads and horns are visible. The upward curves of these intertwined black horns form a strange design, recalling the steeply curving roofs of the pagodas.

Léon Werth, *Cochinchine*

LEFT
Mekong Delta: fresh water is transported in jars between the nipa palms and mangroves.
OVERLEAF
Central Vietnam: a fisherman pulls up his net in the Hoi An River.

Ferrymen hold a special place in the provinces of Vietnam. There are so many canals and rivers and not enough bridges, so often the only way to get across is to go by boat. There are now car ferries that link the major routes, enabling cars and trucks to cross. But on the smaller rivers, people rely on the small boats that the ferrymen or ferrywomen row in their own style, whether with a single paddle, a pair of oars or even moving the oars with their feet.

LEFT
Ferry on an Annamese river in the early twentieth century. · Painting on glass: the tomb of Tu Duc in Huê. · A ferryman on the Saigon River, working the oars with his feet. · Central Vietnam, Thua Tiên Huê province: daily life on the sampans. · Woodcut: riverside pavilion.

INSET
Rowers on the Bang Giang River, in the province of Cao Bang, in Tonkin (Chinese border) · Fishermen at Don Son in Tonkin. · Fishermen at Qui Nhon in Annam. · Painted plaster decoration from a pagoda entrance; the carp symbolizes long life.

RIGHT
South Vietnam: bathing on a sampan.

254

Once the children are ready, Mrs Huong sets off in her skiff on a branch of the Perfume River. She is leaving to paddle close to the quay that runs beside the Lê Loi Boulevard, a stone's throw from the big hotels. With her three words of English, she offers to take tourists on a boat trip along the river. She does not sing the traditional boatmen's shanties like the sampan-owners of the past, nor does she wear the *ao dai*: just a *baba*, loose pyjamas that women wear as work clothes. Mrs Huong wants her daughter to do well at school, so that one day the family will be able to live on land and have a more secure future. As for her daughter, she lives cosily inside the boat. She loves the round roof of the sampan, feeling her brothers and sisters clinging to her, rocked by the waves. In the evening, she dreams of the river fairies as she listens to the water lapping softly against the hull.

LEFT
Huê: early morning on a sampan in the Perfume River.
RIGHT
The Perfume River: the family ducks do not stray far from the family boat.

A floating market in the Mekong Delta. In the village of Cai Rang, a few platforms are raised above the water. The houses stand on stilts; the villagers chose the point where the rivers meet as the site of their marketplace. The floating market, held on barges, sampans or rowing boats, offers a range of local produce, including limes, shrimps, and both sea and freshwater fish. In their rowing boats, housewives come to do their daily shopping. All the services that the market traders need are available on the water: one boat sells noodle soup, another offers sandwich rolls, and the boat that sells drinks doubles as a telephone booth.

LEFT
Huê: daily life in a sampan on the Perfume River.
RIGHT
Floating market in Cai Rang, in the Mekong Delta.

The Hoi An River has changed the destiny of the city that now bears its name. Formerly known as Fai Fo, Hoi An was once a port but for centuries it has been unable to accommodate ships. Sand and silt carried down by the river were pushed inland by the strong currents of the sea, blocking access to the port. But the docks still exist, behind the homes of the wealthy Chinese merchants who have contributed to the city's fortunes. Their solid architecture, influenced by the seafarers' native cultures, has now become a tourist attraction, turning this port city into a living museum. Thousands flock here every year to admire the loveliest city in Vietnam, the pearl of the Hoi An River.

LEFT
Preparing dinner on a sampan in the Hoi An River.
RIGHT
The former Hoi An docks have been converted into restaurants and tourist cafés.

Burdened with the silt stripped from its banks, the clays that tinted it crimson as if the red setting sun had drowned in it, the Red River rolled along, wide and expansive, pushing its fertile waters to the foot of the embankments, sometimes sluggish, sometimes ready to burst its banks. And without beginning or end, just like the river, the intangible spirit that inhabited it was drawn along too.

Yveline Féray, *Dix Mille Printemps* (Ten Thousand Springs)

Some bridges are as famous as the rivers they span. Some symbolize an era or an historic event, like Hanoi's Doumer Bridge (now the Long Biên Bridge) or the USSR–Vietnam Friendship Bridge (now the Thang Long Bridge). Huê boasts Stone Bridge, the Thanh Toan House Bridge and the Truong Tien Bridge, its riveted metal curves designed by Gustave Eiffel.

LEFT
Hanoi: sampans and floating homes along the banks of the Red River. •
Huê: balloon-seller on the Truong Tiên Bridge which spans the Perfume River.
• Mekong Delta: schoolchildren arriving by ferry near Cân Tho.
RIGHT
South Vietnam: female dockworkers on the Dông Nai River. • Diên Biên Phu: Thai women crossing a bridge over the Nam Youn River. • Mekong Delta: the 'monkey bridge', a flimsy structure of bamboo and mangrove wood; children play on it, cross it on their way to and from school and use it as a diving board.

The Vietnamese are drawn to their rivers, where they become lost in contemplation. Returning to the source, to the flow of existence, the powerful current of the water: these images haunt their thoughts and dreams. As they perform their morning exercises, facing the water, their flowing arm movements are like question marks drawn in the air. Do the waters clear their minds? Are they looking into the distance or seeing more clearly inside themselves? Is it destiny that asks questions, or simply the flow of the water?

PRECEDING PAGES
Central Vietnam: a meander of the Thu Bôn River near Da Nang.
LEFT
Fishermen on the Perfume River.
RIGHT
Hanoi, Lake Hoan Kiêm: morning exercises in the shade of the flame trees.
OVERLEAF
Hanoi: couples share a romantic moment beside the Western Lake.

ACKNOWLEDGMENTS

All my thanks to Jean-Louis Marzoratti, Jean-Claude Pomonti, Yann Legoff, Christian Merer, Alain Freynet, Hubert Ollié, Pham Hai Anh and Vanina Sopsaisana.

Thanks also to all those I met on my travels through Vietnam:
M. An, Anh Tho, Bao Ngoc and Les, Bich Hau, Binh, Châu, Chien Thang, Dinh Nam, Do Hai, Dung Beo, Hai Bang, Hang, Hoa, Hoang Ha, Hoang Son, Hong Nhung, Hop, Huy Loc, Huynh Hoa, Mme Khanh Nam Kieu Van, Lân, Lâp, Liên, Ly, Mai Huong, Manh Sinh Manh Tuan, Minh Hanh, Minh Tri, Ngoc Lan, Ngoc Son, Nhu Mai, Ong Viêt, Phuong Lan and Denis, Phuong Liên, Quyen, Quynh Hoa, Sy Ha, Thach, Thanh Lam, Thanh Mai, Thanh Viêt, Thu & Linh, Thuy Hoa, Tu An, Van Song, Viêt Duc, Vinh, Xuân Giap, Xuan Khanh.

BIBLIOGRAPHY

Further reading
Mark Ashwill and Thai Ngoc Diep, *Vietnam Today: A Guide To A Nation At A Crossroads*, Intercultural Press, Boston, 2005.
Justin Corfield, *The History of Vietnam*, Greenwood Press, Portsmouth, NH, 2008.
Neil James, *Understanding Vietnam*, University of California Press, Berkeley, CA, 1995.
Nhung Tuyet Tran and Anthony Reid (eds), *Viet Nam: Borderless Histories*, University of Wisconsin Press, Madison, WI, 2006.
D. R. Sardesai, *Vietnam: Past and Present* (4th ed.), Westview Press, New York, 2005.
Keith Taylor, *The Birth of Vietnam*, University of California Press, Berkeley, CA, 1991.
Vu Dinh Dinh, *Selected Vietnamese Poetry*, R & M, Stafford, TX, 2001.
Shelton Woods, *Vietnam: An Illustrated History*, Hippocrene Books, New York, 2002.

Works quoted
p. 28 Hoang Ngoc Phach, *Un Coeur pur*, Gallimard, Paris, 2006.
p. 38 Duong Thu Huong, *Paradise of the Blind*, HarperCollins, New York, 1991.
pp. 53 & 249 Léon Werth, *Cochinchine*, Éditions Viviane Hamy, Paris, 1997.
pp. 66 & 147 Roland Dorgelès, *On The Mandarin Road*, Century, New York and London, 1926.
p. 77 Yvonne Schultz, *Le Sampanier de la baie d'Along*, Kailash, Paris, 1995.
p. 100 Norman Lewis, *A Dragon Apparent*, Eland Publishing, London, 2003.
p. 109 Thich Nhat Hanh, *No Death, No Fear: Comforting Wisdom for Life*, published by Rider. Reprint by permission of The Random House Group Ltd.
p. 125 Nguyên Huy Thiep, *Conte d'amour un soir de pluie*, Éditions de l'Aube, La Tour d'Aigues, 1999.
p. 134 F. M. Savina, *Histoire des Miao*, Hong Kong, 1924.
p. 154 Nguyên Khac Vien and Huu Ngoc, *Mille Ans de littérature vietnamienne. Une anthologie*, Philippe Picquier, Arles, 1996.
p. 178 Carolijn Visser, *Voices and Visions: A Journey Through Vietnam Today*, trans. Susan Massotty, Sycamore Island Books, Boulder, CO, 1994.
p. 189 Duong Thu Huong, *No Man's Land*, Hyperion East, New York, 2005.
p. 204 Pierre Schoendoerffer, *The Paths of the Sea*, trans. Patrick O'Brian, Collins, London, and Coward, McCann & Geoghegan, New York, 1977.
p. 220 Philippe Franchini, *Continental Saigon*, Editions Métailié, Paris, 1995.
p. 227 Graham Greene, *The Quiet American*, Vintage, London, 1955.
p. 260 Yveline Féray, *Dix Mille Printemps*, Philippe Picquier, Arles, 1996.

To Xuân Diêu, Thao and Luu

DESIGNS USED FOR THE CHAPTER OPENINGS
The bronze drums of Dong Son date from the fifth century BC to the third century AD and are typical of the Dong Son civilization of the Red River basin in North Vietnam. They are cylindrical in shape with a curved 'cushion' at the top; the sides are fitted with hooks from which they can be suspended. Used in rain-making ceremonies, these drums were also symbols of power and could be used to summon warriors into battle. The surface has a central star-shaped motif, which would be struck with a hammer. The surrounding decoration consists of concentric circles filled with a variety of detailed depictions of birds, frogs, warriors, dancers, boats, geometric shapes, and more.

PHOTO CREDITS

© Hachette Photo Library
p. 70 bottom right; p. 96 bottom right; p. 132; p. 150 top; p. 150 bottom; p. 151 left: Hué; p. 151 right; p. 224 right; p. 239; p. 252 top left.

© Vérascopes Richard/Hachette Photo Library
p. 21 top left: Tetterel; p. 21 top right: de Batz; p. 21 bottom right: Dr Le Lan; pp. 42–43 top: Dr Guillon; p. 43 centre left: Moreau; p. 43 centre right: Colonel Diguet; p. 51 right: de Batz; p. 70 top right: Nacher; p. 70 centre left: Laguesse; p. 70 bottom right: Roullet; p. 96 top right; p. 96 top left: Dr Le Lan; p. 127 left: Colonel Diguet; p. 127 right: Colonel Diguet; p. 190 top right: Nacher; p. 190 bottom right: Delacouralle; p. 190 top left: Dinthillac; p. 201: Voisin; p. 202: Voisin; p.s 202–203 top: Javal; p. 203 left: Brissac; p. 203 right: Voisin; p. 224 left: Diguet; p. 230: Dr Le Lan; p. 252 bottom left: Javal; p. 252 centre left: Colonel Diguet; p. 252 centre right.

Translated from the French by Josephine Bacon, American Pie

First published in the United Kingdom in 2009 by
Thames & Hudson Ltd, 181A High Holborn, London WC1V 7QX

www.thamesandhudson.com

Original edition © 2007 Editions du Chêne - Hachette Livre
This edition © 2009 Thames & Hudson Ltd, London

British Library Cataloguing-in-Publication Data
A catalogue record for this book is available from the British Library

ISBN 978-0-500-28785-9

Printed and bound in China